W9-BTI-950

Outstanding Dissertations in Bilingual Education, 1980

Recognized by the National Advisory Council on Bilingual Education

BRIAR CLIFF COLLEGE
LIBRARY

SIOUX CITY, IOWA

NATIONAL CLEARINGHOUSE
FOR BILINGUAL EDUCATION

LC
3731
.O95

This document is published by InterAmerica Research Associates, Inc., pursuant to contract NiE 400-80-0040 to operate the National Clearinghouse for Bilingual Education. The National Clearinghouse for Bilingual Education is jointly funded by the National Institute of Education and the Office of Bilingual Education and Minority Languages Affairs, U.S. Department of Education. Contractors undertaking such projects under government sponsorship are encouraged to express their judgment freely in professional and technical matters; the views expressed in this publication do not necessarily reflect the views of the sponsoring agencies.

Permission to reproduce this material has been granted by the authors and/or publishers to the National Clearinghouse for Bilingual Education and InterAmerica Research Associates, Inc. Requests for reproduction permission should be directed to the respective authors and/or publishers.

InterAmerica Research Associates, Inc. d/b/a
National Clearinghouse for Bilingual Education
1300 Wilson Boulevard, Suite B2-11
Rosslyn, Virginia 22209
(703) 522-0710 / (800) 336-4560

ISBN: 0-89763-055-6
First printing 1981
Printed in USA

10 9 8 7 6 5 4 3 2 1

6603220

Contents

Foreword v

Panel of Judges, 1980, Outstanding Dissertations. vi

Members of the National Advisory Council on Bilingual
Education vii

Levels of Citizen Participation in Selected ESEA Title VII
Bilingual Education Advisory Committees: An Exploratory
Study of Power Relationships between Community Clients
and School Authorities
Rudy Rodríguez, First Place 1

The Construction and Validation of the Listening and
Reading Components of the English as a Second Language
Assessment Battery
María Lombardo, Second Place 23

The Development and Measurement of Syntactic and
Morphological Variables in the Written Spanish of
Native Spanish-speaking Students in Fourth to Ninth
Grades
Ema T.J. Paviolo, Third Place 45

The Relationship of Bilingual Bicultural Education and
Regular Education in the Verbal and Nonverbal Performances
of Chicano Students
Frank Z. Alejandro, Semifinalist 59

A Psycholinguistic Analysis of the Oral Reading Miscues
of Selected Field-Dependent and Field-Independent
Native Spanish-speaking, Mexican American First
Grade Children
Arlinda Jane Eaton, Semifinalist. 71

Mexican American Culture in Bilingual Education Classrooms
Grades 1 through 3: A Description of Three Spanish/English
Programs in Texas
Paul Franklin Gonzales, Semifinalist 87

The Relationship of Language Orientation and Racial/Ethnic
Attitude among Chinese American Primary Grade Children
Irene Sui-Ling Kwok, Semifinalist 99

The Performance of Bilingual Children on the Spanish
Standardized Illinois Test of Psycholinguistic Abilities
Frederich McCall Pérez, Semifinalist 109

A Comparison of Achievement of Mexican American Children
in the Areas of Reading and Mathematics when Taught
within a Cooperative and Competitive Goal Structure
Juanita L. Sánchez, Semifinalist 121

Aspira v. Board of Education of the City of New York:
A History and Policy Analysis
Isaura Santiago Santiago, Semifinalist 137

Foreword

Outstanding Dissertations in Bilingual Education contains summaries of ten dissertations recognized by the National Advisory Council on Bilingual Education in 1980. The material presented in this book marks the second year of this competition and represents a growing body of diverse scholarship in the field of bilingual education.

In 1978 Alfredo de los Santos, a member of the National Advisory Council on Bilingual Education, proposed that the council recognize distinguished research in bilingual education by sponsoring an Outstanding Dissertations Competition. De los Santos developed rules and procedures for the competition based on guidelines formulated by other professional organizations such as the International Reading Association, the Council of Community College Professors, and the American Psychological Association. Winners of the 1980 competition were formally announced at the annual meeting of the National Association for Bilingual Education in Anaheim, California, 16-24 April 1980.

One of the activities of the National Clearinghouse for Bilingual Education is to publish documents addressing the specific information needs of the bilingual education community. We are proud to add this distinguished collection of papers to our growing list of publications. Subsequent Clearinghouse publications will similarly seek to contribute information which can assist in the education of minority culture and language groups in the United States.

National Clearinghouse for Bilingual Education

Panel of Judges, 1980
Outstanding Dissertations
National Advisory Council on
Bilingual Education

Alfredo G. de los Santos, Jr., Chair
Vice Chancellor for Educational
  Development
Maricopa Community Colleges
Phoenix, Arizona

Joe R. Burnett
Dean, College of Education
University of Illinois at Urbana-
  Champaign
Urbana, Illinois

Antonio Simoẽs
Professor
Columbia University
New York, New York

Russell N. Campbell
Department of English
University of California
Los Angeles, California

Theresa H. Escobedo
Assistant Professor
University of Texas
Austin, Texas

Francis T. Villemain
Dean, School of Education
San Jose State University
San Jose, California

Rosa Castro Feinberg
Associate Director
National Origin Desegregation
  Assistance Center
University of Miami
Coral Gables, Florida

Members of
the National Advisory Council
on Bilingual Education

Russell N. Campbell
Department of English
University of California
Los Angeles, California

Robert G. Fontenot
Director
Bilingual Center
University of Southwestern
  Louisiana
Lafayette, Louisiana

Nilda L. García
Director
Evaluation, Dissemination, and
  Assessment Center
Austin, Texas

Richard A. Gresczyk
Office of Indian Education
Minneapolis Public Schools
Minneapolis, Minnesota

Carmen Maldonado
New York Board of Education
Bronx, New York

Ernest J. Mazzone
Director
Bureau of Transitional Bilingual
  Education
Massachusetts Department of
  Education
Boston, Massachusetts

María Sanchez
Hartford Board of Education
Hartford, Connecticut

Paul Sandoval
Senator
Colorado State Legislature
Denver, Colorado

Robert Underwood
Director
Bilingual Training Program
University of Guam
Agana, Guam

Gloria Zamora
Inter-Developmental Research
  Associates
San Antonio, Texas

Levels of Citizen Participation in Selected ESEA Title VII Bilingual Education Advisory Committees: An Exploratory Study of Power Relationships between Community Clients and School Authorities

Rudy Rodríguez

First Place, Outstanding Dissertations
National Advisory Council on Bilingual Education

Degree conferred May 1979
University of New Mexico
Albuquerque, New Mexico

Dissertation Committee:
Richard E. Lawrence, *Chair*
Paul Resta
Ignacio Córdova

About the Author

Dr. Rudy Rodríguez is Director of ESEA Title VII Bilingual Programs and Associate Professor in the Department of Curriculum and Instruction at Texas Woman's University, Denton, Texas. On a Fulbright-Hays assignment in Mexico during spring 1981, he assisted two universities (ENEP Acatlan of UNAM and Monterrey Technical Institute, Mexico City) in planning and conducting training programs for teachers and administrators. Dr. Rodríguez's main interest is in the areas of educational administration, program development, teacher education, and bilingual multicultural education; his experience includes teaching in secondary and adult education programs in Texas, Michigan, and New Mexico, and directing adult and bilingual education programs in Texas. Among his publications is "Citizen Participation in Title VII Programs, An Inquiry into the Impact of a Federal Mandate," in *Bilingual Education and Public Policy in the United States,* edited by R.V. Padilla (Ypsilanti, Mich.: Eastern Michigan Press, 1979).

SUMMARY

The major purpose of the study was to determine the degree to which parent-citizen participation had been achieved in fifteen Texas ESEA Title VII Advisory Committees. An attempt was made in the research to compare levels of citizen participation planned by school officials with those expected by the U.S. Office of Education (USOE) and the federal courts. Through the application of a five-level typology developed at the Recruitment and Leadership Training Institute (RLTI), it was found that school authorities would develop low levels of formal participation, e.g., Placation, Sanctions, Information, employing the RLTI scale, where the pressures from USOE and the courts were low. An escalation in the administrative plans for participation was recorded where the level of the participating step envisioned by these external political institutions was high, e.g., Checks and Balances, according to RLTI. The investigator was able to demonstrate through the RLTI typology that at no point was a high level of participation fully accomplished. The study helped to develop an understanding of Easton's theoretical concepts of support for the authorities and the regime which affected the propensity of the schools to achieve accountable representation toward communities.

STATEMENT OF PURPOSE

An important outcome of the political activity by low-income and minority citizens during the late 1950s and early 1960s was the enactment of the Elementary and Secondary Education Act (ESEA) of 1965. Subsequent amendments to the legislation called for the participation of the community in programmatic decisions. In keeping with the requirements contained in the government mandate, citizen advisory committees were installed in school districts with bilingual programs funded under Title VII of ESEA.

The primary purpose of the study was to provide descriptive data on the forms and characteristics of parent-citizen participation in ESEA Title VII programs, with a particular focus on the exertion of citizen power over program administration vis-à-vis advisory committees. A five-level typology posited by the Recruitment and Leadership Training Institute (RLTI) at Temple University was used in the study as the basic analytical tool for making distinctions among levels of formal participation. RLTI defined each level of the typology as follows:

1. *The Placation [Level]*—School officials and school boards allow community persons and parents to ... make whatever minimum decisions [are] necessary to keep the noise level down. The "noise" may be generated from various sources—the federal government, state level agencies....

2. *The Sanctions [Level]*—The major purpose is to find persons, preferably highly visible to the widest community, who will give sanction to already established or newly developed school goals.

> The choice of citizens who ... participate is left solely to ... school officials or board members.... Participants are selected to serve various predetermined ends, in general, to spread the word of approval concerning goals which remain largely shaped by school officials themselves.

3. *The Information [Level]*—The major purpose is to bring together a group of persons who have information which school officials have decided they need or which they have been directed to obtain by, e.g., the federal government or their own board. The... school officials maintain control over the choice of persons who will participate .... When programs are involved, the school officials must locate and bring together persons whom the programs are designed to serve. It is assumed that the participants have information (which the school officials lack in some measure) about what needs those programs should be designed to meet, [what] services those programs should offer, and what features should be avoided.

4. *The Checks and Balances [Level]*—The major purpose of this [level] is to provide citizens or some segment of them with some inquiry, veto, and "checkmate" powers.... The model necessitates a two-way exchange of information between citizens and school officials, and citizens must approve or disapprove certain decisions regarding programs they have been gathered together to protect and foster in their own interest.

5. *The Change-Agent [Level]*—... The major purpose is to set in motion a series of events that will assure that the group, as individuals and as a collective, and the substance with which they are dealing, will change over a period of time. The changes must be goal-oriented in terms developed by the participants.... In this model citizens have what might be called "negative power" [to prevent things] but they also have "forward motion power" through the new roles they develop.[1]

A corollary facet of the research included an examination of the administrative representational styles of ESEA Title VII project directors, i.e., the extent to which the directors were committed to honoring community-client interests in their professional decisionmaking. Three styles of administrative representation were defined by Mann:

> The *trustee representative* persists in following his/her own judgment even when he/she knows that the action is contrary to the expressed wishes and interests of the people being represented.

> The *delegate representative* believes that he/she has been chosen to reflect accurately (not to interpret or replace) what the client systems say they want and need.

> The *politico representative* responds to representational issues on occasions as a delegate and, on other occasions, as a trustee.[2]

DEFINITION OF TERMS

For the purposes of the study, the following definitions of terms and concepts were applicable:

- *Community client system:* Citizens who live and work within the boundaries of a school district and are served by that district. Parents of school children are subsystems of the client system.

- *Citizen participation (or involvement):* A means whereby a community of persons plays some active role in governance of their own affairs for the purpose of assuring a government that is more responsive to their needs and wishes. Citizen participation mechanisms do not, in terms of legal sanctions, supplant the established government authority, i.e., the board of education. Citizen participation may be demonstrated either through direct input to the educational decisionmaking process or through representatives.

- *ESEA Title VII Advisory Committee:* A continuing formal organization of citizens and professionals mandated by federal law for the purpose of assisting school officials in decisions related to the development, implementation, and evaluation of Title VII bilingual education programs.

- *School authorities:* School district personnel with legal power to create and/or administer policy decisions. For the purpose of this study, four major groups of school authorities were considered: members of boards of education, superintendents, principals, and project directors of bilingual education.

CONCEPTUAL BASE

The concepts of power and decisionmaking which explicitly undergird the RLTI typology have inspired much of the current research on the politics of education. According to Rosenthal, politics, power, and decisionmaking are inextricably related. He further maintains that the investigation of educational decisionmaking is the means for locating educational power. In this perspective, power is defined

> ...as the relative ascendency or predominance of one individual or group over others, with regard to particular values, resources, or objectives.[3]

Easton (in his analysis of political systems) referred to these values as cultural mechanisms that regulate whether citizens' wants will be converted into demands in a political system, e.g., the school system.[4] More specifically, Minar viewed citizen participation as a quality of the political culture or ethos, "...as emerging in the first instance from the values and attitudes citizens have concerning how politics ought to be conducted."[5]

This perspective has found support in several studies on school-community relations.[6] Ethnicity, sex, and socioeconomic status of a community can influence the character of community demands made of school authorities and the way these authorities respond. Similarly, the socioeconomic status of a community influences its organizational resources and its ability to mobilize demands.

Easton believes that, in contrast to citizen attitudes toward political participation, the extent to which governmental structures embrace citizen participation influences the character and quantity of demands flowing into the political system.[7] Racism, paternalism, chauvinism, and resistance by school officials to power redistribution are cultural mechanisms (as defined by Easton) that can deter citizen groups from genuine participation.

Political scientists have defined politics as "the struggle of men and groups to secure the authoritative support of government for their values."[8] In the same vein, García persuasively argues that

> groups and organizations, constructed along economic, social, occupational, religious, and cultural lines, are the primary actors in the U.S. political system.[9]

This contemporary view of politics has helped to provide a more realistic approach to the study of political influences in education. Studies on the policy-making structures of educational systems may thus consider questions that could not be analyzed usefully with conventional concepts of politics, i.e., partisanship and elections.

RESEARCH PROCEDURES

Fifteen ESEA Title VII Advisory Committees in Texas public schools were scrutinized to determine the extent and significance of community client participation in programmatic decisionmaking. (See Table 1 for descriptive characteristics of study sample school districts.) A self-selected sample of twenty-eight school districts originally identified for the study was further reduced to the aforementioned fifteen districts in an attempt to generate a sample which would closely resemble the larger aggregate of Texas Title VII Advisory Committees (n=42). The fifteen study sample committees were compared with the state population of committees on three important characteristics: ethnicity of committee members; type of committee membership, e.g., parent/nonparent characteristic of members; and sex.

The exploratory nature of the investigation necessitated a data-collection plan that was structured enough to direct the study toward its goals but flexible enough to allow for the inclusion of other pertinent data. To meet these specifications, four data-collection techniques were employed as part of a convergence of evidence strategy; i.e., confidence was placed in those findings which were identified in two or more data sources. The data-collection instruments used in the study were tested for content validity and reliability and found to be adequate for the purpose of the study. The acquisition of the relevant data was accomplished through a two-phase design.

Phase I data were obtained directly from members of study sample committees (n=263) through a mail survey conducted during the spring semester of the 1976–77 school year. Based on a 46.7 percent average return rate from each study sample district, the fifteen Title VII committees were classified in relation to the five levels of citizen participation described by RLTI.

Phase II data were acquired through a review of records of Title VII programs in the study, e.g., federal proposals, interim and final evaluation reports, and onsite interviews with the Title VII project directors and randomly selected committee members. Materials examined as part of the records review process covered eight years. A total of sixty committee members (an average of four members per district) and thirteen project directors were interviewed during the onsite visitations. The interview

Table 1
Descriptive Characteristics of Study Sample
Title VII Programs and Committees

School District	FY 1976 Title VII Level of Funding	Number of Years in Force	Title VII Student Enrollment	Demographic Characteristics	RLTI Committee Role
A	$135,495	2	1,650	Urban	Placation
B	82,754	5	290	Rural	Placation
C	88,748	7	460	Urban	Placation
D	117,187	6	250	Rural	Placation
E	152,635	3	425	Rural	Sanctions
F	102,528	2	410	Rural	Sanctions
G	151,848	7	1,030	Rural	Sanctions
H	84,167	3	343	Rural	Sanctions
I	400,000	7	2,900	Urban	Sanctions
J	201,053	7	833	Rural	Information
K	143,543	6	675	Urban	Information
L	468,291	8	1,756	Urban	Information
M	425,916	7	2,104	Urban	Information
N	400,000	6	1,203	Urban	Information
O	159,915	3	615	Rural	Information

Source of Data: Dissemination Center for Bilingual Bicultural Education, *Guide to Title VII ESEA Bilingual Bicultural Projects in the United States* (Austin, Tex.: DCBBE, 1976).

survey of committee members yielded an 80 percent response rate as seventy-five members were originally scheduled for this part of the study. Two of the fifteen Title VII project directors were not available for interview, having resigned their position with the district.

Phase II of the study had a two-fold purpose: (1) to verify the accuracy of data collected in Phase I, and (2) to acquire other data relevant to the problem of the study that were not included in the preliminary phase of the investigation.

AN ANALYSIS OF THE FEDERAL REQUIREMENTS FOR CITIZEN PARTICIPATION IN ESEA TITLE VII PROGRAMS

Before discussing the findings of the study and, in particular, the way administrators put the concept of citizen participation delineated in the ESEA Title VII legislation into operation, it is important to understand the objectives of the legislation. Once this conceptual background and political context are known, it becomes easier to understand how and why local administrators acted as they did.

In this preliminary facet of the research, it was found that the evolution of formal citizen participation in the Title VII programs could be conceptualized as having occurred in three major stages in accordance with the RLTI typology: Placation/Sanctions, Information, and Checks and Balances. (See Figure 1.) It should be recalled that much of the original social and education legislation enacted during the 1960s coincided with the larger emphasis on poverty and civil rights—two issues that were particularly popular during President Johnson's administration. Consequently, citizen participation as it evolved in the federal programs of the 1960s was seen "as merely one aspect of the broader need for improving the livelihood of . . . the poor, the less educated, and racial and ethnic minorities."[10] More ominously, these "culturally disadvantaged" groups were viewed by the early program planners as individuals with little education and few skills, who presumably had little to offer their children. As for the children, they were ". . . lacking motivation for school and were products of limited backgrounds."[11]

Implicit in the early attempts to involve "have-not" Chicanos, Blacks, Puerto Ricans, and other disenfranchised U.S. minorities was not the intent to enable people to participate in planning or conducting programs, "but to enable power holders to educate or cure the participants."[12] A statement contained in the "Metropolis Public Schools'" (a pseudonym for the school district) 1968 Title I proposal epitomized this "therapeutic" involvement of the poor:

> . . . it is hoped that [the parent involvement program] may instill in parents a more positive attitude toward education and evoke in them a healthy and worthwhile attitude toward increased motivation, help, interest, attention, and supervision of children.[13]

Inasmuch as the original federal regulations for parental involvement issued by the newly formed division of bilingual education in 1968 called for the installation of advisory committees in school districts with Title VII programs, at the heart of these directives was an interest to promote a compensatory model of education (as described in the "Metropolis Schools'" Title I proposal). It should also be mentioned that, while the advocacy efforts of bilingual education proponents for significant levels of community involvement during the early years of the Title VII legislation were laudable, the drive during the 1960s to eliminate poverty prevailed in shaping the goals and objectives of programs designed for the so-called disadvantaged citizenry. Also noteworthy was that the requirements for community involvement lacked a solid legal base, since this activity was not initially mandated by federal law. Rather, these requirements were contained within the government directives and guidelines issued by USOE for the operation of federally funded programs. This apparent impotence of federal legislation combined with the strong antipoverty sentiment of the country suggests that Title VII program officials may have tacitly expected a compensatory mode of community activity in bilingual programs. Ostensibly, involvement of parents in decision making was not necessarily a government priority in the early bilingual programs, which suggests the Placation or Sanctions level of participation.

In the April 1971 guidelines for Title VII, school authorities were required to consult with parents and other community members in planning the bilingual program. For example, it was stated in these guidelines that

> needs cannot be adequately assessed without consultation with the parents and community representatives, the people who have "been there" and who live with first-hand knowledge of their children's problems in an English-speaking environment. Nor can long-range

Figure 1
Stages of Citizen Participation Based on Administrative Regulations and Guidelines for ESEA Title VII Programs Between 1968 and 1978 as Defined in the RLTI Typology

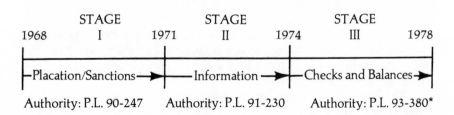

*Requirements for community involvement were not officially mandated by the U.S. Congress until 1974, through P.L. 93-380. Previous directives for formal participation issued by USOE through its administrative regulations and guidelines did not carry the power of law.

goals be postulated without the knowledge of parents' aspirations for their children. Without the active support of the parents and the community, the goals will be inadequately achieved and plans will contain hidden pitfalls.[14]

It appears, therefore, that an escalation in the level of community participation in bilingual programs was envisioned by USOE in comparison to earlier requirements. The new posture by USOE suggests that community advisory committees were expected to function in accordance with the Information participatory model described by RLTI. The same guidelines also placed emphasis on involvement which reflected and strengthened parent and community support for bilingual education.

Public Law 93-380, passed by the U.S. Congress in 1974, suggested an increased level of participation by community clients in bilingual education. Inasmuch as this law and the subsequent regulations issued by USOE mildly encouraged parent-citizen participation in many roles, e.g., as paid paraprofessional and volunteer aide, government officials emphasized parent-citizen involvement in decisionmaking. Prompted by a major interest at the federal level "to combat the ills of overly centralized decision making,"[15] USOE, through the authorization contained in P.L. 93-380, issued regulations that required school districts applying for ESEA funds (including Title VII) to "establish an advisory committee for the entire district." In addition, the mandate required that these committees—

a. [have as] a majority of its [committee] members parents of children to be served [by the federal program];

b. [be] composed of members selected by parents in each school district;

c. [be] given responsibility by [the district], for advising it in the planning for, and the implementation and evaluation of, such programs and projects. . .

d. [be] provided by such agency [the district] with access to appropriate information concerning such programs. . . .[16]

School officials were further obligated to hold public hearings on applications for federal assistance prior to their submission to USOE. Funds were made available for parent-clients to attend national, state, and local workshops and conferences. It was apparently felt that community impact on decisions would be strengthened if community members were properly informed of the nature of federally funded programs and related requirements governing their operation.

The amended requirements for ESEA programs, including Title VII, broadened the concept of community participation to bring it closer to involvement strategies found in Head Start, Model Cities, and other federal programs. The new posture assumed by the U.S. Congress in 1974 through P.L. 93-380 reflected the government's interest to endow citizens with power over federally funded programs. While the advisory relationship to administrators described in the 1974 government mandate displayed features of token community representation, it was, nevertheless, much more specific in the expectations and standards it placed on local administrators for compliance. This change in legislative policy further suggests that government officials may have envisioned participation of community groups in ESEA programs in accordance with the Checks and Balances role model defined by RLTI.

SALIENT FINDINGS OF THE RESEARCH

The foregoing discussion provides a backdrop for understanding the actions of school administrators toward formal participation as analyzed in this section. Salient findings of the research are presented here in relation to the three RLTI stages of citizen participation suggested in federal guidelines and regulations for Title VII since the implementation of the original legislation in 1969. (See Figure 1.)

Beginning with the first federal proposals filed by school districts in 1969, local program planners were required to specify how parent and community involvement would be achieved in Title VII programs. In a review of the early proposals for the study sample's bilingual programs which were funded under the 1969 ESEA Title VII legislation (n=6), it was suggested that school district officials may have seen community involvement in a limited way. There appeared to be little demonstrable community involvement in existing bilingual programs—evidence of citizen participation was primarily limited to a display of lists of community "representatives" attending bilingual program meetings called by school officials. These meetings were generally held to inform the community of the bilingual program. Although these data are sketchy, the evidence does tend to suggest that the local district plans for formal participation in the early Title VII programs were in conformity with federal expectations, i.e., Placation/Sanctions level of citizen participation as defined by RLTI.

The extent to which community involvement in bilingual programs was achieved, pursuant to the requirements issued by USOE in 1971, is not altogether clear as data sources other than written records, e.g., interview data with personnel serving in the Title VII programs during the period, would have helped to provide more descriptive data of actual participation. Through application of the RLTI typology, fluctuations in citizen participation were recorded, however, in districts with court-ordered desegregation plans. Five urban districts with desegregation programs mandated by the courts during the years 1971-1974 were identified in the study. These district plans also included provisions for bilingual education. In connection with these programs of desegregation, federal funds were made available to the five urban districts under the Emergency School Assistance Act (ESAA) to support administrative efforts in implementing desegregation plans including bilingual education. Like ESEA Title VII, ESAA required community involvement in program development and implementation. The intensity of the combined pressures of ESEA, ESAA, and the federal courts for meaningful levels of community involvement was clearly evident in the evaluation reports of the study sample districts affected by desegregation. The evaluation reports for a district in east Texas revealed evidence that community client members of ESEA-ESAA Bilingual Advisory Committees were "actively" involved in determining school assignments of Chicano and Black children for purposes of desegregation. In a north-central Texas school district, members of a Bilingual Advisory Committee were selected to serve on a "Tri-Ethnic" Committee appointed by the federal district court to assist in drawing up the desegregation plan for the school system. Another committee of a district affected by court-ordered desegregation assisted in determining the eligibility of schools for bilingual education programs.

The above descriptive data suggest that the level of citizen participation planned by local district officials may have escalated to the Information or Checks and Balances level according to the RLTI typology. It is strongly indicated, furthermore, that administrative officials may have scaled up their plans for citizen participation to comply with the participatory step envisioned by both the courts and USOE.

As the major thrust of the present study was to review the Title VII committees operating during the 1976–77 school year, a more precise assessment of the participatory levels of these groups was possible due to the comprehensive nature of the data-collection design. As previously indicated, the legal base for these committees was contained in P.L. 93-380 as enacted by the U.S. Congress in 1974. According to Phase I and II study findings, four school districts had committees operating at the Placation level; five districts, at the Sanctions level; and six districts, at the Information level. (See Table 1.) At the time of the present investigation no committees were functioning at the level intended by the 1974 federal law, i.e., Checks and Balances as categorized by RLTI.

Typically, members of the Title VII committees in the study sample were of Mexican American origin, female, and parent of a child in bilingual education. (Other descriptive characteristics of the study sample are shown in Table 1.) Furthermore, the level of responsibility considered appropriate for parent-clients in the study sample programs, including the mechanisms established by school officials for participation, did suggest basic differences in the philosophies under which the various programs operated. It was found, for example, that Title VII programs with Placation or Sanctions type committees tended to emphasize community involvement activities that would help the community client assimilate new knowledge and attitudes. This involvement of minority group communities was demonstrated in a statement filed by School District C as part of their 1976 interim evaluation report:

While the efforts of this group (volunteer parent aides) are highly appreciated, they do need definite training in lettering, coloring, operating the duplicating and laminating machines and on techniques on how to work with children. In an effort to solve this, the bilingual-bicultural professional staff plans to help these volunteers improve their skills, techniques and self-confidence.

In District B's Title VII proposal it was reported that

...the bilingual program seeks to develop parents to the end that they become better parents, effective teachers of their own children, and supportive resources of the school.

The foregoing objectives for client involvement affected the types of parental roles encouraged by school officials, including the degree of participation elicited. For example, when asked in the Phase II interview, "What, in your opinion, is the most important contribution your committee has made to the bilingual program?" typical responses from citizen members of the Placation and Sanctions level committees were:

1. Judging a Holiday Spirit Contest

2. Making Christmas decorations

3. Trying to help children get home assistance

4. Assisting in the classroom.

It was suggested, therefore, that the function of the advisory committees classified as Placation and Sanctions was not to advise on the direction of the bilingual program *per se*. The focus was on improving or changing parent behavior. Moreover, the extent to which the community resources were to play a role in the schools was not the prerogative of parent-clients; this was decided by the professionals. This suggests that as formal mechanisms for citizen involvement, Placation and Sanctions type committees were amenable to control by administrators.

Compliance with the community involvement requirements contained in P.L. 93-380 was most nearly achieved by school districts with Information type committees. Citizen participation activities originating from the Information model tended not to assume deficiencies on the part of the community clients constituting the target population of Title VII programs. It was believed, rather, that culturally different clients possessed special knowledge and skills which could effectively be used in the development of the bilingual program. For instance, when asked, "What, in your opinion, is the most important contribution your committee has made to the bilingual program?" a District L committee member remarked:

One thing that has come about because of a committee suggestion is La Feria Estudiantil (the Student Fair), which will be completely bilingual next year. It will involve spelling, art, and music and it will be district-wide.

Another member of the same committee, who taught in the bilingual program, discussed the work of the parents in evaluating Spanish language materials for relevancy of vocabulary to the local community.

In School Districts J, K, N, and O, community rooms having names of special cultural appeal, e.g., El Quiosco and Casa Amigo, were designated in school buildings as a meeting place for parent-clients. These community rooms also served as a work area for parents to make piñatas, cultural costumes for the children, and teaching aids for the classroom.

At this third level of client participation it appears that program planners did listen to citizen insights and altered their plans accordingly— which, according to RLTI, is the primary merit of the Information role model. Moreover, the results of promotional efforts by the advisory committees, including staff members of the bilingual program, were especially noticeable among all Information level projects as illustrated below. The following are selected comments (from the interview survey) by parents and bilingual program personnel in School districts J, L, M, and O:

> The advisory committee has brought a much greater knowledge [to the general community] of the bilingual program, the workings of it, and its goals and objectives.

> I have said before, but this bears repeating—I consider bilingual education to be an elite part of public education.

> Two years ago people did not know why children were learning Spanish. The council helped in spreading the word.

In sum, it can be noted from the preceding discussion that as federal mandates increased the demands for meaningful participation, school districts became less and less willing to write these mandates into their plan. This was especially evident in districts with Placation and Sanctions type committees. It is further apparent that school authorities tended to resist implementation of the formal plans for citizen participation unless external political pressures were sufficiently strong to alter or overcome bureaucratic objections or delays. The pressure exerted by the courts and USOE for a greater degree of formal participation—in connection with issues of desegregation, for example—effected a higher state of citizen involvement according to the RLTI typology. A correspondence is suggested, therefore, between the formal participatory role planned by local school authorities and what they were forced to do by outside pressures. The greater the pressure, the higher the levels of participation planned. Based on this rationale, it can be argued that a decrease in the intensity of pressure from USOE and the courts could have resulted in the scaling down of formal participatory plans by school officials. Consequently, by 1976 four of the five districts affected by the desegregation mandate (initially ordered by the courts in 1971-72) were operating their committees at the Information level.

One district had scaled down its participatory plans to the Sanctions level. These data further suggest that school authorities may have been ignoring or minimizing their school-community relations program in favor of relationships with broader constituencies, i.e., the federal government.

A corollary facet of the inquiry included an examination of the administrative representational style of ESEA Title VII directors, i.e., the extent to which these administrators were committed to honoring expressed community interests in their professional decisionmaking activity. In this regard, Title VII directors were expected by federal regulations to represent the community in a responsive manner. Initial interview data acquired from the directors with the three types of RLTI committees tend to bear out this expectation. These data indicate that the directors in the study sample were receptive to community input in administrative matters and were willing to implement community requests for changes in the bilingual program. In accordance with Mann's three-level interpretation of administrative representation (see page 4), the representational role orientation of the ESEA Title VII directors appears, at first glance, to be consistent with the primary characterization of the delegate representative. Further probing in the interviews, combined with data acquired in the records review and interviews with community members, suggests that the directors were relatively powerless in dealing with the community, despite their claim to having a great deal of authority over community matters related to the bilingual program.

In a school district in central Texas, for example, the project director talked about the "ingenious protections in his programs against militants." According to the director, these provisions had been built into the bilingual program by the area superintendents who wanted the bilingual committee to be composed of citizens supportive of the school programs. Further probing in the interview prompted information from the director which suggested that school administrators were fearful that members of a so-called militant community organization might "infiltrate" the schools. This community group, consisting mainly of Chicanos, had achieved a negative reputation among both city government and school officials for their unconventional pressure-type politics. School officials had expertly devised a checks and balances system in the selection of candidates for the advisory committee involving the building principals, the project directors, and finally, the area superintendents. The director whose committee type was classified as Information confided that:

> Advisory committees will never be effective in any school program unless they become autonomous. As long as the school district controls their composition and functions, they will never be autonomous.

The data thus suggest that despite a basic inclination among the Title VII project directors to honor community interests in their decisionmaking activity, and possible variations in their representational role orientations, control by their administrative superiors prevented them from adequately responding to community interests. A second factor which prevented effective administrative representation of community interests was the socio-economic background of the communities served by the Title VII programs. In three rural school districts, the project directors complained of the poor attendance or inactivity of low-income parent-clients in Title VII committee meetings. In these districts, the project directors had no choice but to use their own ideas about community needs and interests in programmatic decisions. Hence, the Title VII directors reluctantly assumed a trustee representational role according to Mann's definition.

The data indicate, therefore, that the extent to which project directors came to accept a formal role of communities in the decisionmaking process was relatively limited; especially in Placation and Sanctions type programs. Data in the exploratory study do not make it altogether clear why administrative officials in study sample districts tended to regulate the community activities of Title VII project directors. It can only be speculated that it was not in the best interest of the administration to encourage too strong an accountability relationship between the director and the community, since this could reduce the project director's accountability to the administration itself. It is further possible to argue that school officials viewed communities engaged in meaningful participatory activities as a threat to the professional control of the schools. In the final analysis, it is suggested that the conservative posture of school administrators may have posed a crucial barrier to Title VII advisory committees achieving the participatory level envisioned by federal officials in the 1974 ESEA mandate, i.e., Checks and Balances, employing RLTI typology.

DISCUSSION OF FINDINGS
IN RELATION TO EASTONIAN THEORY

The conceptual framework that was used to integrate the study data was Easton's political system analysis. According to Easton, a basic characteristic of a political system is its openness, that is, its responsiveness to conditions existing in its environment which have been converted to political demands by members within the system.

> Thus, phenomena, both physical and social, that occur outside the boundaries of a political system may play ... a crucial role in influencing the manner of interaction within the system and the consequent outputs.[17]

Findings in the research study tend to support this basic characterization of Easton's model. It was found, for example, that factors such as federal court decisions and grants-in-aid programs, e.g., ESEA and ESAA, yield important inputs affecting local district policies (or outputs). Some of the most obvious system changes resulting from the influence of these outside forces, as shown in the research study, include a new awareness of the needs of linguistically and culturally different children and the implementation of appropriate programs, i.e., bilingual education, to meet their educational needs. Of special interest to the study is the effect of federal requirements on the formation of advisory committees consisting largely of individuals who traditionally have been denied meaningful access to decisionmaking processes in education, i.e., the poor and culturally different.

A key question emerging from the investigation is why the stress or environmental pressure placed on school systems with Title VII programs through P.L. 93-380 did not result in a high degree of citizen participation, i.e., Checks and Balances level as envisioned by federal officials. This level was temporarily accomplished only when pressure from USOE was combined with court-mandated requirements for citizen participation in conjunction with school desegregation policies. School authorities were not inclined to raise the level of citizen participation merely because of the pressure they felt from the ESEA Title VII mandate. They altered their behavior only after they were subjected to pressures from the courts and the combined Title VII and ESAA mandates for citizen participation. In view of this finding, one is forced to focus on the *character* of the stress, which was influenced in Easton's parlance by two factors: the support system for the authorities and the support system for the regime. Borrowing from similar findings by Cibulka,

> this distinction between the character of stress and its intensity is significant because it helps us understand the support structures . . . support for the authorities and for the regime . . . which affected the propensity of the [school] system to achieve accountability representation toward local communities.[18]

The study tends to reaffirm the traditional norm of separation of education and politics espoused by conservative educators. School authorities in study sample districts manifested a proclivity for autonomy and insulation from public pressures. As a result, decisionmaking processess in school systems seemed relatively closed to influence from the community.

The political culture (see page 5 for Minar's definition) of community members in the study did not appear to pose a major challenge to the professional autonomy sought by school officials. There were data to suggest that citizens favored the use of persuasive deliberations in the articulation of demands, rather than use of conflict techniques. Generally, clients demonstrated their influence by working cooperatively with professionals, e.g., the Title VII project directors and their staff, who, for the most part, shared a common ethnic background, philosophy, and priorities with the community.

RECOMMENDATIONS

The research was built on the assumption that increased power for citizens in the governance of the schools can help create more effective, responsive schools. In view of this consideration, an overriding recommendation of the study is that objectives for community involvement programs in Title VII programs recognize that parent-clients have special knowledge of their children's cultural and academic needs. In this way, citizens advisory committees can be seen as a means for creating meaningful changes or improvements in school programs designed particularly for linguistically and culturally different learners. Findings in the study regarding programs with Information level committees tend to support this recommendation.

There is little evidence in the research data which indicates that attempts were being made by school districts to train community people to be effective collaborators in educational decisionmaking. Therefore, it is recommended that training programs, such as the one developed by the Leadership Training Institute of the Urban/Rural School Development Project, be implemented in school districts interested in involving community groups in programmatic decisionmaking. This training program involves both professional educators and lay citizens in the process. In general terms, the Leadership Training Institute's Program

> ... utilizes the educational resources available in both the school and the community. . . . The total training package includes activities that help professional staff members and community people develop techniques designed . . . to translate the local situation into educationally relevant programs, i.e., Black studies, Indian education, bicultural education.[19]

Further research that employs the RLTI typology is recommended. The investigation suggests that the typology can serve as a viable analytical tool for assessing levels of citizen participation in education programs. It is therefore recommended that a comparative study be conducted of citizen participation in programs funded by the federal government, e.g., ESEA Title I, Head Start ESAA, Follow Through. This study should be designed to analyze relationships between advisory committees operating at the various levels of the RLTI typology and their subsequent impact on the quality of programs. Attitudinal surveys should be employed to determine the influence of differentiated levels of participation on the behavior of the lay participants, i.e., to what extent participation in advisory committees reduces feelings of powerlessness or alienation among low-income and minority clients. Such a study might also examine particular cultural orientations of minority group citizens and the extent to which these orientations influence the political participation of this group. There are a number of threads running through the data which suggest that the sociocultural experience of Mexican Americans can influence the character of their political participation.

Finally, since the concept of administrative representation has been applied on a very limited basis to educational administration, more research is needed in order to make it a useful analytical tool for practicing administrators. It is recommended, moreover, that the proposed study be conducted across various school systems or federally funded programs. A research focus on the similarities and differences of representational styles of minority and majority group administrators would yield data which could improve the training of administrators for multicultural communities.

CONCLUSION

The exploratory study data presented in this paper may be assessed on the basis of the degree to which the study sample is representative of the larger aggregate of Texas Title VII advisory committees. In this regard, it should be emphasized that a special effort was made to maximize the comparability level of the study sample to the general population of Texas committees. As previously indicated, three characteristics—ethnicity, sex, and parent/non-parent committee membership—were selected as the basis for this comparative analysis. These three characteristics were chosen because of their particular importance and relevance to the study of parent and community participation in programmatic decisionmaking. In judging the applicability of the study results to states outside Texas, one should exercise caution. In this respect, there seemed to be a number of characteristics in the Title VII programs and advisory committees in the sample, e.g., funding level and socioeconomic characteristics of the community, which might also be operative in similar programs and committees in other states.

While there are some inherent limitations to the study primarily because of its exploratory design, it supports the value and utility of theoretical application to data acquisition and analyses. Easton's analysis of political systems, with its sensitivity to the interactions of political systems with the environment, was especially useful in the analyses and organization of the study data. For this writer, as for Wirt and Kirst,

> the utility of systems theory is that of all heuristic schemes—it enables us at least to order existing knowledge or hunches and thereby to determine what portions of the scheme are clearly untenable, which ones have at least some support, and which need to be further studied.[20]

The increasing trend toward citizen participation in governmental programs presents a need for research tools that are capable of assessing the extent and significance of this activity. The RLTI typology, which focuses on the power relationships between citizens and authorities, may prove useful in this assessment process.

NOTES

1. Recruitment and Leadership Training Institute, *Community Parity in Federally Funded Programs*, a report prepared for the U.S. Office of Education National Center for the Improvement of Educational Systems (Philadelphia, Pa.: Temple University, 1971).

2. Dale Mann, *The Politics of Administrative Representation* (Lexington, Mass.: Lexington Books, 1976).

3. Alan Rosenthal, *Introduction to Governing Education: A Reader on Politics, Power, and Public School Policy*, ed. Alan Rosenthal (Garden City, N.Y.: Anchor Books, 1969), p. x.

4. David Easton, *A Systems Analysis of Political Life* (New York, N.Y.: John Wiley and Sons, Inc., 1965), p. 86. Easton defines citizen *wants* as expressions of interests, opinions, expectations, and preferences. *Demands* are wants that constituent groups, e.g., community clients and the federal government, express toward administrators for authoritative action.

5. David W. Minar, "The Community Basis of Conflict in School System Politics," *American Sociological Review* 31 (December 1966), pp. 9822-34.

6. For example, see Robert K. Yin et al., *Citizen Organizations: Increasing Client Control over Services* (Santa Monica, Calif.: Rand Corporation, 1973).

7. Easton, op. cit.

8. Frederick M. Wirt and Michael W. Kirst, *Political and Social Foundations of Education* (Berkeley, Calif.: McCutchan Publishing Corp., 1975).

9. F. Chris García, "Politics and Multicultural Education Do Mix," *Journal of Teacher Education* 28 (May–June 1977), p. 25.

10. Yin, op. cit., p. 101.

11. Ibid.

12. Sherry R. Arnstein, "A Ladder of Citizen Participation," *American Institute of Planners Journal* 25 (July 1969).

13. James G. Cibulka, "Administrators as Representatives: The Role of Local Communities in Urban School Systems" (unpublished doctoral dissertation, University of Chicago, 1973), p. 212.

14. U.S. Department of Health, Education, and Welfare, *Programs under Bilingual Education Act (Title VII, ESEA) Manual for Project Applicants and Grantees* (Washington, D.C.: Government Printing Office, 1971), p. 1.

15. Yin, op. cit.

16. U.S. Congress, *Public Law 93-380*, 93rd Congress, H.R. 69, 21 August 1974 (Washington, D.C.: Government Printing Office, 1974), p. 14.

17. Easton, op. cit., p. 102.

18. Cibulka, op. cit., p. 198. Support for the regime focuses on the roles, offices, norms, and rules which govern the authorities.

19. James V. Terry and Robert D. Hess, *The Urban/Rural School Development Program: An Examination of a Federal Model for Achieving Parity Between Schools and Communities* (Stanford, Calif.: Stanford University, 1975), pp. 52-54.

20. Wirt and Kirst, op. cit.

The Construction and Validation of the Listening and Reading Components of the English as a Second Language Assessment Battery

María Lombardo

Second Place, Outstanding Dissertations
National Advisory Council on Bilingual Education

Degree conferred September 1979
Boston University School of Education
Boston, Massachusetts

Dissertation Committee:
María Estela Brisk, *Chair*
Thomas E. Culliton
Louis Aikman
Roselmina Indrisano
Celeste E. Freytes

"The Construction and Validation of the Listening and Reading Components of the 'English as a Second Language Assessment Battery'" by María Lombardo has appeared in part in Research Notes of the *TESOL Quarterly*, Vol. 14, No. 2 (June 1980), copyrighted 1980 by Teachers of English to Speakers of Other Languages. This material is used by permission.

About the Author

Dr. María Lombardo is Assistant Professor in the Department of Reading and Language at Boston University, and Language Assessment Coordinator/ Field Application Specialist at the Bilingual Resource Training Center there. She has published and presented numerous papers on developing language assessment procedures and on language, cognitive, and reading development among various bilingual groups in native and second language settings. Her other professional activities include developing and organizing minicourses, workshops, and technical assistance for bilingual and English as a second language teachers on such topics as assessment procedures, legislation, and instruction in first and second language reading; and teaching university courses on diagnosing abilities and achievements of bilingual students and on bilingual and Italian reading.

SUMMARY

This study was intended to provide bilingual classroom teachers with an effective, criterion-referenced instrument, the English as a Second Language Assessment Battery (ESLAB), for assessing the receptive (listening and reading) and the expressive (speaking and writing) language areas of secondary limited-English-speaking students. The battery consists of an Oral Screening Test, Oral Competency Test, Aural Comprehension Test, Structural Competency Test, Informal Reading Inventory (IRI), and Writing Sample. To validate the battery and ascertain its statistical stability three teacher training workshops were conducted, then a sample of fifty-nine Hispanic inner city secondary students (twenty-five boys and thirty-four girls aged twelve to sixteen) was tested. From the results, test items were analyzed and revised. Validity of the tests was determined by having language and reading experts examine and evaluate the tests and by comparing the tests' results with students' English as a Second Language (ESL) grades, performance on other standardized tests, and teacher estimates. Overall, the tests seemed to be accurate predictors of how students would perform in ESL and reading classes. Reliability, determined through statistical analysis, showed the ESLAB to be dependable in that the instrument would produce similar results were it to be administered time and time again. Test results also indicated interrelationships within and between the receptive and expressive language areas.

STATEMENT OF THE PROBLEM

In bilingual education a major concern is that of assessing the English language proficiency of the secondary bilingual students once they are identified as having limited English proficiency under Title VII or according to the Lau Categories. The latter place students in the following classifications:

1. Monolingual speakers of the language other than English (speaks the language other than English exclusively)

2. Predominantly speaks the language other than English (speaks mostly the language other than English, but speaks some English)

3. Bilingual (speaks both the language other than English and English with equal ease)

4. Predominantly speaks English (speaks mostly English, but some language other than English)

5. Monolingual speaker of English (speaks English exclusively).

(U.S. Office of Civil Rights: Task Force Findings, 1975, p. 2)

Diagnosis of language proficiency, essential in grouping secondary limited-English-speaking students for instruction in bilingual programs, has been problematic for four reasons:

1. Inconsistent identification of specific language proficiency skills for functioning in a unilingual *or* bilingual classroom (Cummins, 1979)

2. Nonspecification of proven reliable and valid norm- or criterion-referenced tests that measure linguistic competencies of secondary bilingual students in the native language (L_1) and second language (L_2) (Silverman, Noa, and Russell, 1977)

3. Limited availability of criteria for grouping bilingual students for ESL and reading instruction

4. Lack of evidence as to interrelationships among listening, speaking, reading, and writing as these areas relate to secondary bilingual students.

PURPOSE OF THE STUDY

To address these pedagogical concerns, the intent of this research was to construct and validate an effective, reliable criterion-referenced instrument, the English as a Second Language Assessment Battery (ESLAB), for assessing the receptive (listening and reading) and the expressive (speaking and writing) language areas of students learning English as a Second Language (ESL) in bilingual education programs. The validation of the ESLAB was divided into the review of the Receptive and Expressive Language Areas based on the facts that individuals acquire competence before performance and that the Receptive Area precedes the Expressive Area in the acquisition of language (Horowitz and Berkowitz, 1967; Chastain, 1976; Marshall and Glock, 1978). This study focused on the construction and examination of the Receptive Area, which included the Aural Comprehension Test, the Structural Competency Test, and the Informal Reading Inventory. It established the reliability and validity of these test components and assessed their value as potential instruments for grouping bilingual students in ESL and reading classes. Additionally, results from the Oral Screening Test, the Oral Competency Test, the Dictation Exercise, and the Writing Sample were analyzed to note interrelationships between the receptive and expressive language areas.

DEFINITION OF TERMS

For purposes of this study the following terminology is used:

- *Aural Comprehension:* The student's listening functional reading level.

- *Bilingual:* A person who is in a two-language environment, regardless of how little he or she can communicate in the second language (Zintz, 1975, p. 428).

- *Bilingual Education:* A program utilizing the student's native language for developing skills and concepts according to his or her age level, while also teaching English skills.

- *Bilingual Student:*

   1. A pupil of a non-English-speaking background who has been classified according to the Lau categories as eligible for bilingual education.

   2. A pupil in a bilingual education program.

- *Domain:* A cluster of social situations which are typically constrained by a common set of behavioral rules (Fishman, 1972).

- *Home Language:* The language used in the home.

- *Language:* A highly complex system of conventional oral symbols by means of which members of a community interact for the purpose of communication (Silverman, Noa, and Russell, 1977, pp. 17-18).

- *Language Different:* A student whose language is other than English.

- *Language Proficiency:* The degree to which an individual demonstrates his or her linguistic competence in a language, regardless of how that language may have been acquired (Jones and Spolsky, 1975, p. 2)

- *Language Dominance:*

   1. The primary language in which a child interacts most often; the language used in the home (U.S. Office of Civil Rights: Task Force Findings, 1975).

   2. The comparison of skills in two or more languages (Zirkel, 1976, pp. 323-30).

- *English-Speaking:* A student whose home language is English.

- *Native Language:* The language that a person acquires in early years and that normally becomes his or her natural instrument of thought and communication.

- *Non-English Speaker:* A student whose home language is other than English and who has little or no knowledge of oral English.

- *Oral Comprehension:* The individual's ability to derive meaning from a language as spoken by native speakers (Gutiérrez and Rosenbach, 1975, p. 3).

- *Reading:* The ability to derive meaning from the graphic form of the language (Gutiérrez and Rosenbach, 1975, p. 4).

- *Reliability:* How accurately a test measures whatever it is intended to measure (Thorndike and Hagen, 1969, p. 177).

- *Speaking:* The ability to produce the sounds of the language and to combine these sounds into meaningful utterances (Gutiérrez and Rosenbach, 1975, p. 3).

- *Unilingual:* Monolingual speaker of one language (U.S. Office of Civil Rights: Task Force Findings, 1975).

- *Validity:* Whether a test measures what it is intended to measure (Thorndike and Hagen, 1969, p. 163).

  1. Concurrent validity—determined by evaluating the results of a given test with those of standardized measures or other external criteria.

  2. Content validity—based on experts' opinion (Nelson, 1974) as to whether the test items truly measure the objectives they purport to measure (Edmonston and Randall, 1972).

  3. Face validity—based on examiner and examinee judgements.

  4. Predictive validity—established by comparing tests' results against indicators of students' actual performance in a given area (e.g., report card grades). According to Edmonston and Randall (1972) instruction and mastery of test items should be equivalent.

NEED FOR LANGUAGE PROFICIENCY
ASSESSMENT OF BILINGUAL STUDENTS

The current concern for language proficiency assessment of bilinguals has evolved from various interrelated issues: (1) the fact that non-English speakers have been haphazardly placed into programs for the mentally retarded, based on instrumentation that has not been normed for this population and, consequently, (2) the resulting low achievement for these individuals placed in sink-or-swim situations through submersion in total English programs, and (3) compliance by educators with bilingual legislation emphasizing English language proficiency as a primary variable in bilingual programs.

The first issue has been substantiated by a longitudinal study (Mercer, 1971), which found that in one school 32 percent of the 81 percent Anglos, 45 percent of the 11 percent Mexican Americans, and 21 percent of the 8 percent Blacks were placed in classes for the mentally retarded based on results from standardized measures. The reason for this not uncommon situation is the inherent danger of cultural and linguistic bias in utilizing instrumentation that was not normed with the group making use of such tests (Condon, 1975; Morishma and Mizokawa, 1977).

The misuse of testing instruments and the placement of limited English speakers leads to the second issue of concern, that of continual low achievement and high dropout rates (Samora, 1968; Sánchez, 1971). High dropout rates have been reported for Mexican Americans, Puerto Ricans (U.S. Commission on Civil Rights, 1971-1976), and Native Americans (U.S. Commission on Civil Rights, 1978). Negative achievement rates have also been noted for other linguistic minority groups (Coleman, 1966; Task Force on Children Out of School, 1970; *Lau* v. *Nichols*, 1974; National Assessment of Educational Progress, 1977). The 1977 National Assessment of Educational Progress has reported that the educational achievement of linguistic minority students is "constantly below the achievement of the total national age population" (p. 5).

In acknowledgment of these perplexing statistics the government passed the Bilingual Education Act of 1968. The mandate of bilingual legislation is that instruction has to be in the minority students' native language (L_1) (U.S. Office of Education, 1976) and that students' language needs in their native language and English (L_2) must be met to prepare these students for participation in English curriculums (*Lau* v. *Nichols*, 1974; U.S. Office of Civil Rights: Task Force Findings, 1975). The Educational Amendments of 1978 stressed that the students to be serviced in bilingual education programs are those ". . . who have difficulty speaking, reading, writing, or understanding the English language . . ." (p. 70). Compliance with legislation on the part of educators leads to the third issue, the identification of language proficiency instruments designed for bilingual students. The problem is that although numerous formal and informal tests exist (Gutiérrez and Rosenbach, 1975), they are seldom comprehensive or organically interrelated in design.

THEORETICAL FRAMEWORK

Based on the crucial need for a uniform procedure in the assessment of English language proficiency skills of limited English speakers, the English as a Second Language Assessment Battery (ESLAB) was developed. Cohen's model (1975) (Figure 1) was used as the theoretical base because it (1) described the receptive (listening and reading) and the expressive (speaking and writing) language areas; (2) indicated that components constituting the language areas that require mastery of phonemes and graphemes, familiarity with vocabulary (lexicon), internalization of grammatical structures or rules of language usage (syntax), attaching meaning to referents (semantics), and applying sequences of linguistic components to the broader context of experience (pragmatics) (Oller and Kyle, 1978); (3) depicted the language domains or contexts within which language can be described; (4) indicated the language variety or the type of language (Fishman, 1972) that is used in diverse geographical locations or within the same speech community or communities; and (5) highlighted all of these elements as critical in L_1 and L_2 development.

Although Cohen (1975) presented one model of language, inter-relationships of the four language areas (listening, speaking, reading, and writing) have been viewed and studied in various ways. Many experts have noted that oral language, or listening and speaking, precedes written language or reading and writing (Loban, 1963; Ruddell, 1965; Taylor, 1969; Bradley, 1970; Smith, 1971; Ingram, 1974; Goodman, 1976; Ruddell, 1976; Carline and Hoffman, 1976). In addition, the receptive language areas

Figure 1
Language Areas

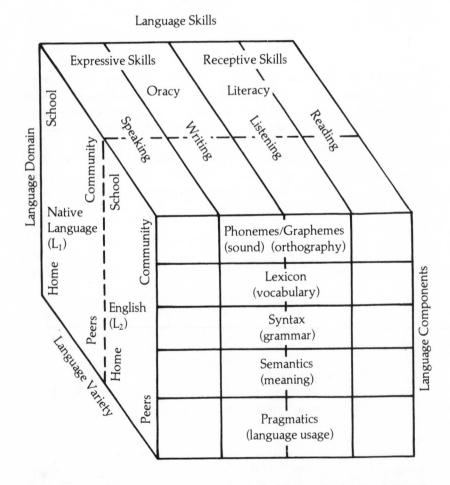

Adapted from Cohen (1975).

(listening and reading) were found to be parallel to the expressive language areas (speaking and writing) (Chastain, 1976; and Horowitz and Berkowitz, 1967).

For the purpose of this study, listening and reading were examined in greatest detail. Many researchers are in accord that listening and reading correlate with each other (Devine, 1968; Carroll, 1970; Wilkinson and Stratta, 1979; Wilkinson, 1971; Murray, 1972; Massaro, 1977). Yet other experts have indicated that, although related, listening and reading require different skills (Goodman, 1976; Wilkinson and Stratta, 1970; Murray, 1972; Schallert, Kleinman and Rubin, 1977; and Stoltz and Portnoy, 1978).

With the establishment of a theoretical framework, the most important considerations in assessing language are the areas to be assessed and the methods for assessing them. The notion of what is to be assessed can be addressed by reviewing the controversial areas of language competence v. performance, language proficiency v. communicative competence, and language dominance v. language proficiency.

Chomsky (1965) differentiated between an individual's internalized knowledge of vocabulary, the rules (grammar) for joining words together that constituted competence, and an individual's observable language output, or his or her performance or production (McNeill, 1966; Wilkinson, 1971). Although in many instances testers examine competency through an individual's language performance, it should be noted that performance does not always reflect competence.

In the ESLAB, competence was tested before performance. Listening and reading (Receptive Language Area) as indicators of competency preceded speaking and writing (Expressive Language Area) as indicators of performance.

Communicative competence (Oller and Conrad, 1971) can be measured through the observation of an individual's actual use of oral language in a functional situation. Language proficiency is the evaluation of a person's degree of oracy (listening and speaking) and literacy (reading and writing) skills (MacNamara, 1969; Jones and Spolsky, 1975).

A distinction between language dominance and proficiency is that *dominance* (Dickson, 1975; Zirkel, 1976) refers to an individual's oral communicative competence (U.S. Office of Civil Rights: Task Force Findings, 1975) while language *proficiency* takes all the language skills into consideration. For the ESLAB, proficiency was the primary concern.

The issue of how language is to be assessed can be explained through existing philosophies (discrete point and integrative) and the possible instruments (norm and criterion referenced) to be considered in language assessment. Traditionally, the discrete point approach, which assessed an individual's ability to manipulate the individual components of language, was utilized. More recently, however, integrative assessment, which allows for examination of students' global language abilities in a holistic manner, has been employed (Oller, 1975; Shuy, 1978; Oller and Kyle, 1978). For the ESLAB, a combined approach of discrete-point and integrative philosophies was adopted.

Language proficiency can be measured through either norm-referenced or criterion-referenced tests. Norm-referenced tests tend to provide a global idea about student performance (Popham et al., 1973), since the intent of these tests is to establish normative reference groups. Scoring criteria are not determined until all subjects have completed a given test and a mean has been calculated (Glaser and Nitko, 1971; Popham and Husek, 1971; Randall, 1972; Oakland, 1972; Smith, 1973; and Popham et al., 1973).

On the contrary, criterion-referenced tests outline specific behavioral objectives and establish a priori scoring criteria in order to determine students' mastery or nonmastery of content. The concern is to isolate the individual's strengths and weaknesses so that followup instructional objectives can be delineated (Jackson, 1970; Roudabush, 1971; Blatchford, 1971; Davis, 1971; Randall, 1972; Edmonston and Randall, 1972; Smith, 1973; and Popham et al., 1973).

Variability is the essential validity issue between norm- and criterion-referenced tests (Popham and Husek, 1971). Because the purpose of a norm-referenced test is to compare a group of individuals with objective criteria, it is expected that subjects' performance would vary over a wide range. However, in the case of a criterion-referenced test individuals are compared to a specific performance standard (Nitko, 1971; Popham and Husek, 1971). Therefore, it may be the case that the scores of a group of students taking a criterion-referenced test could fall within close range of each other. This would not indicate lack of validity on the part of the test but that most of the students had mastered given content or skills. For the purpose of this study, a criterion-referenced battery of tests was developed based on specific behavioral objectives.

The major consideration in the development of the ESLAB was to provide for (1) the possible varying levels of L_1 and L_2 abilities among bilingual students, (2) the fact that some students may or may not have world knowledge (Cummins, 1979), (3) the fact that others may or may not have aural/oral skills in L_1 or L_2, and (4) the fact that still others may or may not be literate in L_1 and/or L_2. To accommodate these levels, the administration of a native language test prior to the ESLAB is recommended, since research studies agree that in most cases students possessing competence or literacy skill in L_1 are capable of transferring such skills to L_2 (Orata, 1953; Vásquez and Barrera, 1953; Castro de la Fuente, 1961; Arnold, 1968; Burns, D., 1968; Modiano, 1968; Pryor, 1968; Hillerich and Thorn, 1969; Taylor, 1969; Wise, 1969; Burns, N., 1970; Ehrlich, 1971; Inclan, 1971; John, Horner, and Berney, 1971; Dubé and Hebert, 1975; Rosier and Farella, 1976; USAID, 1967). Then the ESLAB is administered to examine English (L_2) skills through aural/oral, reading, and writing tests. Once results are attained students are grouped into five entry level categories (Beginner I and II; Intermediate I and II; and Advanced) for instruction.

ANALYSES OF DATA

The validation procedure for the Receptive Language Area of the ESLAB included item analysis, establishment of reliability, and the confirmation of test validity.

Item Analysis

Researchers question conventional item analysis for criterion-referenced tests (Thorndike, 1967; Thorndike and Hagen, 1969; Popham and Husek, 1971; Litchman, 1973; and Sax, 1974). Yet they are not clear as to the appropriate procedure for criterion-referenced items (Litchman, 1973). For the ESLAB, item analysis was based upon the test developer's judgement of item relevancy and empirical data results.

The data results for the Receptive Language Area were as follows:

1. Aural Comprehension Test: p (percentile, difficulty index) values ranging from 27.1 percent to 89.9 percent and RPB (point-biserial correlation, discrimination index) values of .08 to .67

2. Structural Competency Test: p values of 1.7 percent to 64.4 percent and RPB values of -.01 to .47

3. Informal Reading Inventory (IRI): p values between 0.0 percent and 69.5 percent and RPB scores of 0.0 to .70

The trend was that items were either simplistic or extremely difficult, as in the case of the latter two tests. However, when students' overall performance was examined there was an indication of mastery of oral/aural skills but not of literacy skills.

Reliability

Reliability was attained statistically based on Hoyt and Cronbach alpha (Neslon, 1976) values of internal consistency. The calculated estimates of reliability were as follows: Aural Comprehension Test, Hoyt Estimate, .81; Structural Competency Test, Hoyt value, .37; and IRI, Hoyt value, .83. The values for the Aural Comprehension Test and the IRI were acceptable in each case being over .70 (Thorndike and Hagen, 1969), but the estimate for the Structural Competency Test was extremely low. A possible reason for the low value is that the majority of students did not attempt the test, yet the ones that did (in most cases the high achievers of the overall ESLAB) performed badly, thus creating disharmony to the internal consistency of the test. The low reliability of the Structural Competency Test, in turn, inflated the SEM of 4.25 for the Receptive Area. Total test statistics were also calculated. For the three tests the Hoyt value was .79 and Cronbach's coefficient was .21, and the IRI Hoyt estimates for the individual stories ranged from .31 to .71 with an overall Hoyt of .83 and Cronbach's coefficient of .74.

Validity

Validity was of four types. The first, face validity, indicated that both examiners and examinees viewed the test positively. In terms of the second type, content validity, language and reading experts analyzed the test items in terms of specified objectives. Based on their judgments, items were altered accordingly. The third, predictive validity, used Kendall's tau (Nie et al., 1975) to correlate each test component's level results (Beginner I, Beginner II, Intermediate I, Intermediate II, and Advanced) with the four Teacher Estimates (TE) of how each student would perform on the ESLAB, and the students' ESL report card grades (see Table 1). The resulting indices indicated a positive, significant relationship among the three variables. The fourth was concurrent validity used only for the IRI. A Pearson coefficient indicated a high correlation between the following indicators: the IRI and Cloze Test, 7484 at $p < .01$; IRI and *Stanford Diagnostic Reading Test* (1976 Edition), .6203 at $p < .01$; Stanford and Cloze .6105 at $p < .05$; TE and Stanford .4248 at $p < .05$; TE and Cloze .3577. The three reading tests were related but the IRI and TE had a negative (-.4056) relation since teachers tended to underestimate students' levels.

From these results, it was concluded that the Receptive Area tests are valid measures of language proficiency.

Interrelations of the Language Areas

The data also served to demonstrate interrelationships among the language areas (Oller, 1975) or the contentions that (1) within the Receptive Language Area, listening and reading are related; (2) the language areas of listening, speaking, reading, and writing are interrelated, with the components of the Receptive Area having the same relationship as those of the Expressive Area, and the components of oral language having the same relationship as those of written language; and (3) oracy skills precede literacy skills. To examine these relations raw scores and level results (Beginner I, II; Intermediate I, II; Advanced) for the seven tests were plotted on Pearson Correlational Matrices.

Raw scores of the Receptive Area tests indicated no relationship between the Aural Comprehension Test, the Structural Competency Test, and IRI. However, each test had a high correlation, .6050, .3730, and .8090 at $p < .01$, respectively, with the total test score. The explanation may be that these tests were related to the Receptive Language Area but may, in fact, have been examining different skills.

Level results of the Receptive Area indicated a close relationship between listening and reading abilities with values of .4147 at $p < .01$ for the

Table 1
Predictive Validity Correlations Between Level Performance on the Receptive Language Area Tests, Teacher Estimates and ESL Grades

	Aural Comprehension Test (A.C.)	Structural Competency Test (S.C.)	Informal Reading Inventory (IRI)	English as a Second Language (ESL) Grade
Aural Comprehension				.37662**
Structural Competency				.25200**
Informal Reading Inventory				.37600**
Teacher I (A.C.)			.25899*	.41850**
Teacher I (S.C.)		.33405	.25874*	
Teacher I (IRI)				.35967**
Teacher II (A.C.)		.35714*	.28360*	
Teacher II (S.C.)		.48658**	.32880**	.37693**
Teacher II (IRI)		.57050**	.34568**	.24301*
Teacher III (S.C.)		.32931**		.29860**
Teacher III (IRI)		.34397**		
Teacher IV (A.G.)		.65049**	.50581**	

Note: n = 59.
*$p < .05$.
**$p < .01$.

Aural Comprehension Test and the Structural Competency Test; .3534 at $p < .01$ for the Aural Comprehension Test and the IRI; and .5137 at $p < .01$ for the Structural Competency Test and the IRI.

Correlations for the raw score results of all the ESLAB tests were as follows: Oral Screening Test and Oral Competency Test, .6337 at $p < .01$; Oral Screening and IRI, -.2775 at $p < .01$; Dictation Exercise and Writing Sample, .4157 at $p < .01$; and IRI and Writing Sample, .4046 at $p < .01$. The two oral tests were related and may, in fact, have examined similar skills. The Oral Screening and IRI had a negative correlation since both examined different skills with the first treating oral language and the latter, written language. The two writing tests appeared to be testing similar skills, and the Writing Sample was related to the IRI in that they both evaluated literacy skills.

The relationships for the level results of the ESLAB were as follows: Oral Competency Test and Aural Comprehension Test, .3740 at $p < .01$; Oral Competency Test and Structural Competency Test, .3350 at $p < .05$; Oral Competency Test and IRI, .5057 at $p < .01$; Aural Comprehension and Structural Competency, .4147 at $p < .01$; Aural Comprehension Test and

IRI, .3534 at $p < .01$; Dictation Exercise and Structural Competency Test, .4039 at $p < .01$; Dictation Exercise and IRI, .3276 at $p < .01$; Dictation Exercise and Writing Sample, .2579 at $p < .05$; Structural Competency Test and IRI, .5137 at $p < .01$; and IRI and Writing Sample, .2340 at $p < .05$.

The resulting interrelationship of the Oral Competency and the Aural Comprehension Tests indicates that both measure listening skills. The Aural Comprehension and the Structural Competency Tests both examine similar grammatical structures. The Aural Comprehension Test and the IRI demonstrate a relationship because they are both components of the Receptive Area of Language. The similarity between the results of the Dictation Exercise and Oller's (1975) findings seem to be the primary component to correlate with most of the other ESLAB components. The reason may be that the process of dictation involves listening and then writing, which would incorporate oral and written as well as receptive and expressive language areas. The significant relationship between the Structural Competency Test and the IRI is logical, in that both tests require reading skills. The relationship between the IRI and the Writing Sample indicates that both examine literacy skills. Overall, the components of the Receptive and Expressive Language Areas of the ESLAB seem to be related.

Generally, results indicate a close relationship between listening and reading within the Receptive Language Area. There is also a relationship between the oral language areas, listening and speaking, similar to Oller's (1975) findings. The reading and writing areas also seem to be related.

CONCLUSIONS AND IMPLICATIONS

The significance of this study is threefold: (1) information is provided about the methodology for constructing and validating a criterion-referenced assessment battery; (2) the English as a Second Language Assessment Battery (ESLAB) has been prepared and pilot tested with secondary bilingual students; and (3) the data support the contentions that there are interrelationships among the language areas.

In addressing the first point, the construction of a language battery involves various major considerations. A theoretical framework must be developed. The skills or objectives to be tested have to be outlined. An approach (integrative or discrete point) for assessing skills must be specified, and test types (norm- or criterion-referenced) must be decided. The tests then need to be validated with the population for whom they are intended.

The second factor is that the ESLAB provides classroom teachers with a language profile of bilingual students' listening, speaking, reading, and writing skills. The battery identifies students' Independent, Instructional, and Frustration reading levels, and it groups students into five entry-level categories (Beginner I, II; Intermediate I, II; and Advanced) for ESL and reading instruction. This type of initial assessment is a uniform procedure for providing continuity among bilingual classes and it facilitates organized record keeping of student results.

The third factor is that information about the mastery of language skills and the interrelationships of the language areas was also attained for secondary bilinguals. The trend was that students mastered aural/oral skills before reading and writing skills. It was noted that listening, speaking, reading, and writing are related, but because they require different skills, they need to be tested discretely and integratively. The implication for teachers is that these language areas need to be taught separately and integratively.

Recommendations for the followup of this study are for (1) field testing the ESLAB with other language groups and (2) constructing and validating batteries in other languages so that L_1/L_2 language profiles can be prepared for bilingual students, based on the notion that students may have varying degrees of proficiency in the native and second language.

REFERENCES

Arnold, R.D. *San Antonio Language Research Project 1965-66 (Year 2) Findings.* ERIC ED 022 528, 1968.

Blatchford, C.H. *A Theoretical Contribution to ESL Diagnostic Test Construction.* Paper presented at the Fifth Annual TESOL Convention, New Orleans, March 1971. ERIC ED 013 371, 1971.

Bradley, R.N. "A Study of the Relation of Oral Language Proficiency and Reading in a Group of Fourth Grade Negro Children of a French Linguistic Background." ERIC ED 046 618, 1970.

Burns, D.M. "Bilingual Education in the Andes of Peru." In *Language Problems of Developing Nations,* edited by J.A. Fishman, C.A. Ferguson, and J. Das Gupta. New York: John Wiley and Sons, 1968.

Burns, N. "Materials for the Bilingual Schools of Ayacucho." *Notes on Literacy* 9 (1970): 15-19.

Carline, D.A. and Hoffman, J.R. "Comparison of Language Experience Approach to Reading with a Conventional Reading Approach in Eight Summer Migrant Schools." ERIC ED 135 557, 1976.

Carroll, J.B. "The Nature of the Reading Process." In *Theoretical Models and Processes of Reading,* edited by H. Singer and R. Ruddell. Newark, Del.: International Reading Association, 1970.

Castro de la Fuente, A. *La alfabetización en lenguas indígenas y los promotores culturales.* Mexico, D.F.: Instituto Lingüístico de Verano, 1961.

Chastain, K. *Developing Second Language Skills: Theory to Practice.* Chicago: Rand McNally, 1976.

Chomsky, N. *Aspects of the Theory of Syntax.* Cambridge, Mass.: MIT Press, 1965.

Cohen, A.D. *Redwood City Program in a Socio-Linguistic Approach to Bilingual Education.* Rowley, Mass.: Newbury House, 1975.

Coleman, T. *Equality of Educational Opportunity.* Washington, D.C.: U.S. Government Printing Office, 1966.

Condon, E. "The Cultural Context of Language Testing." In *Papers in Language and Testing,* edited by L. Palmer and B. Spolsky. Washington, D.C.: Teachers of English to Speakers of Other Languages, 1975.

Cummins, J. "Linguistic Interdependence and the Educational Development of Bilingual Children." *Review of Educational Research* (1979): 1-65.

Davis, F.B. "Criterion-referenced Tests." Paper presented at the annual meeting of the American Educational Research Association, New York, February 1971. ERIC ED 050 154, 1971.

Devine, T.G. "Reading and Listening: New Research Findings." *Elementary English* 45 (March 1968): 346-348.

Dickson, D. "The Goals and Problems of Language Dominance Testing." *Materiales en Marcha* (1975): 10-16.

Dubé, N.C., and Hebert, G. *Evaluation of St. John Valley Title VII Bilingual Education Project,* Madawaska, Maine, 1975. Mimeographed.

Edmonston, L.P., and Randall, R.S. "A Model for Estimating the Reliability and Validity of Criterion-referenced Measures." Paper presented at the annual meeting of the American Educational Research Association, Chicago, April 1972. ERIC ED 065 591, 1972.

Ehrlich, A. *Bilingual Teaching and Beginning School Success.* ERIC ED 077 279, 1971.

Fishman, J. *Sociolinguistics: A Brief Introduction.* Rowley, Mass.: Newbury House, 1972.

Glaser, R., and Nitko, A. "Measurement in Learning and Instruction." In *Educational Measurement,* edited by R. Thorndike. Washington, D.C.: American Council on Education, 1971.

Goodman, K.S. "Reading: A Psycholinguistic Guessing Game." In *Theoretical Models and Processes of Reading,* edited by H. Singer and R.B. Ruddell. Newark, Del.: International Reading Association, 1976.

Gutiérrez, M., and Rosenbach, J. *Bilingual Assessment Test Development and Reviews: A Manual for Teacher Use.* Albany, N.Y.: State Education Department, 1975. Mimeographed.

Hillerich, R.L., and Thorn, F.H. *ERMAS: Experiment in Reading for Mexican-American Students.* ERIC ED 035 526, 1969.

Horowitz, M.W., and Berkowitz, A. "Listening and Reading, Speaking, and Writing: An Experimental Investigation of Differential Acquisition and Reproduction of Memory." *Perceptual and Motor Skills* 24 (1967): 207-215.

Inclán, R.G. *An Updated Report on Bilingual Schooling in Dade County, Including Results of a Recent Evaluation Conference on Child Language.* Chicago, November 1971.

Ingram, D.E., and Elias G.C. "Bilingual Education and Reading." *RELC Journal* 5 (1974): 64-76.

Jackson, R. *Developing Criterion-referenced Tests.* ERIC Clearinghouse on Tests, Measurement, and Evaluation, Princeton, N.J., 1970. ERIC ED 041 052.

John, V.P.; Horner, V.M.; and Berney, T.D. "Story Telling: A Study of Sequential Speech in Young Children." In *Basic Studies in Reading,* edited by H. Levin and J.P. Williams. New York: Basic Books, 1971.

Jones, R.L., and Spolsky, B. *Testing Language Proficiency.* Arlington, Va.: Center for Applied Linguistics, 1975.

Karlsen, B.; Madden, R.; and Gardner, E.F. *Stanford Diagnostic Reading Test.* New York: Harcourt, Brace, Jovanovich, 1976.

Lau v. Nichols, 414 U.S. 563. *The U.S. Law Week Supreme Court Opinions* 42 (1974): 4165-4168.

Litchman, M. *The Development and Validation of R/EAL, an Instrument to Assess Functional Literacy.* ERIC ED 081 811, 1973.

Loban, W.D. *The Language of Elementary School Children.* Research Report No. 1. Champaign, Ill.: National Council of Teachers of English, 1963.

MacNamara, J. "How Can One Measure the Extent of a Person's Bilingual Proficiency?" In *Description and Measurement of Bilingualism,* edited by L.S. Kelly. Toronto: Canadian National Council for UNESCO, 1969.

Marshall, N., and Glock, M. "Comprehension of Connected Discourse: A Study into the Relationships Between the Structure of Text and Information Recalled." *Reading Research Quarterly* 14, No. 1, (1978-79): 10-56.

Massaro, D. "Reading and Listening." *Technical Report No. 423.* Madison, Wisc.: University of Wisconsin, 1977. ERIC ED 149 329, 1977.

McNeill, D. "Developmental Psycholinguistics." *The Genesis of Language: A Psycholinguistic Approach.* Cambridge, Mass.: MIT Press, 1966.

Mercer, J. "The Labeling Process." Paper presented at John F. Kennedy Center for the Performing Arts, Washington, D.C., October 1971.

Modiano, N. "Bilingual Education for Children of Linguistic Minorities." *América Indígena* 28, No. 2 (1968): 2.

Morishima, J., and Mizokowa, D. *Testing and Evaluating Asian American/Pacific Islander Bilingual Students.* Tacoma, Wash.: Bilingual Technical Assistance Center, 1977.

Murray, J.G., Jr. "A Study of the Effect of Simultaneous Auditory Visual Presentation at Differentiated Rates on Listening and Reading Comprehension. Unpublished dissertation, Boston University, 1972.

National Assessment of Educational Progress. *Hispanic Student Achievement in Five Learning Areas: 1971-1975.* Washington, D.C.: U.S. Government Printing Office, 1977.

Nelson, L.R. *Guide to LERTAP Use and Interpretation.* Ontago, New Zealand: University of Ontago, 1974.

Nie, N.H.; Hull, H.; Jenkins, J.G. et al. *Statistical Package for the Social Sciences.* New York: McGraw Hill, 1975.

Nitko, A.J. "A Model for Criterion-referenced Tests Based on Use." Papers presented at the Annual Meeting of the American Educational Research Association, 1971. ERIC ED 049 318, 1971.

Oakland, T. "An Evaluation of Available Models for Estimating the Reliability and Validity of Criterion-referenced Measures. Paper presented at the annual meeting of the American Educational Research Association, Chicago, April 1972. ERIC ED 065 589, 1972.

Oller, J. "Assessing Competence in ESL: Reading." In *Papers on Language Testing, 1967-1974,* edited by L. Palmer and B. Spolsky. Washington, D.C.: Teachers of English to Speakers of Other Languages, 1975.

Oller, J., Jr., and Conrad, C. "The Cloze Technique and ESL Proficiency." *Language Learning* 22, No. 2 (1971): 183-195.

Oller, J.W., and Kyle, P. *Language Education: Testing the Test.* Rowley, Mass.: Newbury House, 1978.

Orata, P.T. "The Iloilo Experiment in Education through the Vernacular." In *The Use of Vernacular Languages in Education, Monographs on Fundamental Education VIII.* Paris: UNESCO, 1953.

Popham, J. et al. *Of Measurement and Mistakes.* Testimony before the General Subcommittee on Education, Committee on Education and Labor, U.S.

House of Representatives, Washington, D.C., 29 March 1973. ERIC ED 078 020, 1975.

Popham, J., and Husek, T.R. "Implications of Criterion-referenced Measurement." In *Criterion-referenced Measurement,* edited by W.J. Popham. Englewood Cliffs, N.J.: Educational Technology Publications, 1971.

Pryor, G.C. *Evaluation of the Bilingual Project of Harlandale Independent School District, San Antonio, Texas, in the First and Second Grades of Four Elementary Schools during the 1967–68 School Year, 1968.* ERIC ED 026 158, 1968.

Randall, R.S. "Contrasting Norm-referenced and Criterion-referenced Measures." Paper prepared for symposium of the Annual Meeting of the American Educational Research Association, Chicago, April, 1972. ERIC ED 065 593, 1972.

Roudabush, G.E., and Green, D.R. "Some Reliability Problems in a Criterion-referenced Test." Paper presented at the annual meeting of the American Educational Research Association, New York, February 1971. ERIC ED 050 144, 1971.

Rosier, P., and Farella, M. "Bilingual Education at Rock Point: Some Early Results." *TESOL Quarterly* 10, No. 4 (1976): 379-388.

Ruddell, R. "The Effect of the Similarity of Oral and Written Patterns of Language Structure on Reading Comprehension." *Elementary English* 42, No. 4 (1965): 403-410.

_____. "Psycholinguistic Implication for a System of Communication Model." In *Theoretical Models and Processes of Reading,* edited by H. Singer and R.B. Ruddell. Newark, Del.: International Reading Association, 1976.

Samora, J., ed. *La Raza: Forgotten Americans.* Notre Dame, Ind.: University of Notre Dame Press, 1968.

Sánchez, G.I. "The New Mexican in 1940: A Documentary History of the Mexican-Americans." In *A Documentary History of Mexican-Americans,* edited by W. Meguin. New York: Bantam, 1971.

Sax, G. *Principles of Educational Measurement and Evaluation.* Belmont, Calif.: Wadsworth, 1974.

Schallert, D.L.; Kleiman, G.M.; and Rubin, A.D. "Analysis of Differences between Written and Oral Language." *Technical Report No. 29.* Urbana, Ill.: University of Illinois, 1977.

Silverman, R.; Noa, J.; and Russell, R. *Oral Language Tests for Bilingual Students: An Evaluation of Language Dominance and Proficiency Instruments.* Portland, Ore.: Center for Bilingual Education, Northwest Regional Educational Laboratory, 1977.

Smith, C.W. "Criterion-referenced Assessment." Paper presented at the International Symposium on Educational Testing, The Hague, July 1973. ERIC ED 081 843, 1973.

Smith, F. *Understanding Reading.* New York: Holt, Reinhart, and Winston, 1971.

Stanford Diagnostic Reading Test. See Karlsen et al.

Stoltz, W.S., and Portnoy, S. "Written Communication as Functional Literacy: A Developmental Comparison of Oral and Written Communication." In E.T. Higgins, *Perspectives on Literacy,* edited by R. Beach and P.D. Pearson. Minneapolis, Minn.: University of Minnesota, 1978.

Task Force on Children Out of School. *The Way We Go to School: The Exclusion of Children in Boston.* Boston: Task Force on Children Out of School, 1970.

Taylor, T.E. "A Comparative Study of the Effects of Oral-Aural Language Training on Gains in English Language for Fourth and Fifth Grade Disadvantaged Mexican-American Children." Doctoral dissertation, University of Texas at Austin, 1969.

Thorndike, R.L. "The Analysis and Selection of Test Items." In *Problems in Human Assessment,* edited by D. Jackson and S. Messick. New York: McGraw Hill, 1967.

Thorndike, R.L., and Hagen, E. *Measurement and Evaluation in Psychology and Education.* New York: John Wiley and Sons, 1969.

U.S., Agency for International Development (USAID). "Mother Tongue Literacy and Second Language Learning." In S. Gudschinsky, *Bilingualism in Early Childhood,* edited by W.F. Mackey and F. Anderson. Rowley, Mass.: Newbury House, 1967.

U.S., Commission on Civil Rights. *Ethnic Isolation of Mexican-Americans in Public Schools in the Southwest.* A research report of the Mexican-American study services, Report No. 1. Washington, D.C.: U.S. Government Printing Office, 1971.

U.S., Commission on Civil Rights. *The Excluded Student.* Washington, D.C.: U.S. Government Printing Office, 1972a.

U.S., Commission on Civil Rights. *Reports to the U.S. Commission on Civil Rights on the Education of the Spanish Speaking.* Hearings before the Civil Rights Oversight Subcommittee of the Committee on the Judiciary, U.S. House of Representatives, 92nd Congress, June 1972b.

U.S., Commission on Civil Rights. *The Unfinished Education Outcome for Minority Students in Five Southwestern States.* A research report of the Mexican-American study services. Washington, D.C.: U.S. Government Printing Office, 1972c.

U.S., Commission on Civil Rights. *Social Indicators of Equality for Minorities and Women.* Washington, D.C.: U.S. Government Printing Office, 1978.

U.S., Commission on Civil Rights. *Puerto Ricans in the Continental United States: An Uncertain Future.* Washington, D.C.: U.S. Government Printing Office, 1976.

U.S., Office of Civil Rights. *Task Force Findings Specifying Remedies Available for Eliminating Past Educational Practices Ruled Unlawful under Lau v. Nichols.* Mimeographed. 1975.

U.S., Office of Education, Department of Health, Education, and Welfare. *Bilingual Education: An Unmet Need.* Washington, D.C.: Office of Education Report to the U.S. Congress, 1976.

Vásquez-Barrera, A. "The Tarascan Project in Mexico." In *The Use of the Vernacular Languages in Education* 8, UNESCO Monographs on Fundamental Education, (1953): 77-86.

Wilkinson, A. *The Foundations of Language.* Oxford, England: Oxford University Press, 1971.

Wilkinson, A.M., and Stratta, L. "Listening Comprehension at Thirteen Plus." *Educational Review* 22 (1970): 228-242.

Wise, M.R. "Utilizing Languages of Minority Groups in a Bilingual Experiment in the Amazonian Jungle of Peru." *Community Development Journal* 14, No. 3 (1969): 117-122.

Zintz, M. *The Reading Process: The Teacher and the Learner,* 2nd ed. Dubuque, Iowa: William Brown, 1975.

Zirkel, P.J. "A Method for Determining and Depicting Language Dominance." In *English as a Second Language in Bilingual Education,* edited by J.A. Alatis and K. Twaddell. Washington, D.C.: Teachers of English to Speakers of Other Languages, 1976.

The Development and Measurement of Syntactic and Morphological Variables in the Written Spanish of Native Spanish-speaking Students in Fourth to Ninth Grades

Ema T. J. Paviolo

Third Place, Outstanding Dissertations
National Advisory Council on Bilingual Education

Degree conferred May 1979
The Pennsylvania State University
University Park, Pennsylvania

Dissertation Committee:
Lester S. Golub, *Co-chair*
John B. Dalbour, *Co-chair*
Joseph V. Alessandro
Paul D. Holtzman
Paul D. Weener

About the Author

Dr. Ema T. J. Paviolo, a native of Argentina, is a bilingual/English as a second language (ESL) instructor in the Lebanon (Pennsylvania) School District. In addition to having extensive experience teaching Spanish and ESL at the elementary, secondary, and university levels, she has directed the Title VII Bilingual Program in the Bethlehem (Pennsylvania) Area School District. Dr. Paviolo has written on Spanish Structural Density, a formula to measure native Spanish language development, and on the linguistic characteristics in the written language of native Spanish-speaking students.

SUMMARY

The present study investigated, measured, and provided descriptive information about the developmental characteristics of syntactic and morphological structures found in the written Spanish language samples of native Spanish-speaking students in monolingual (Puerto Rico) and bilingual (Pennsylvania) schools, in fourth to ninth grade.

A stepwise regression analysis based on students' grade levels as criterion measure, and the sums of twenty-one structural linguistic variables counted in two written compositions as predictor variables were tabulated on the data collected in monolingual schools in Puerto Rico. A linear weighted combination of coordinated T-units, sentence adverbials, structure words, compound predicates, and adjectivals significantly correlated with students' grade levels ($p < .01$).

As a measure of cross-validation, an independent population sample consisting of Spanish-speaking students in bilingual education programs in Pennsylvania was also tested. The predictor equation based on the monolingual sample was used to test levels of written linguistic complexity among bilingual Spanish-speaking students. The correlation between predicted values and students' actual grade levels was statistically significant ($p < .001$).

Parallel to the findings revealed by the monolingual sample in Puerto Rico, the bilingual sample in Pennsylvania showed a consistency in the development of linguistic structures with advancing grade levels. The present formula thus derived is a reliable and valid linguistic index that can be used to assess Spanish-speaking students' written native language development according to grade levels.

STATEMENT OF THE PROBLEM

With the implementation of teaching students of limited English proficiency using their native language as a medium of instruction, there has been an increasing concern for minority children's academic progress in both their native and second languages. In order to maintain and improve their level of competence in the second language, English, it is necessary to enable students of limited English-speaking proficiency to raise their level of competence in their native language, as well.

In a Spanish-English bilingual education program, it is important to bring Spanish-speaking students' written language skills close to the level of monolinguals of comparable age and education. Therefore, there seems to be an immediate need for investigating the linguistic structures characteristic of Spanish-speaking students' native language development throughout the school years. By applying this procedure to monolingual and bilingual Spanish-speaking populations, comparisons could be made describing the developmental changes in the process of acquiring linguistic sophistication (maturity).

RATIONALE OF THE STUDY

Educators realize that children write sentences differently as they grow older and progress through school, and that these differences are not only lexical but syntactic and morphological, as well. Yet the specific linguistic structures that native Spanish-speaking children are able to use at different grade levels have not been determined. Likewise, it is not known how often students use certain linguistic structures at each consecutive grade level, what the significant value of each of these structures in the process of written native language development is, nor which of these linguistic variables teachers look for when they evaluate the quality of Spanish writing by native Spanish speakers.

Researchers have been investigating the development of syntax in the English language, trying to find objective, measurable ways to describe the developmental changes in the students' written language through the school years (McCarthy, 1930; LaBrant, 1933; Templin, 1957; Loban, 1963, 1966; Hunt, 1965, 1970; Golub and Frederick, 1970, 1971; Golub, 1973). However, most of the research in Spanish is focused on measuring developmental stages of the oral native language among preschool children (Kernan and Blount, 1966; González, 1970; Brisk, 1972; Toronto, 1972).

A study revealing developmental patterns of written language for Spanish-speaking students in elementary and intermediate grades would be of benefit to educators and linguists, since it could provide the necessary information to identify the most important linguistic variables which are characteristic of linguistic maturity. Such an analysis could be used to enrich Spanish-speaking students' written vocabulary and increase the use of syntactic and morphological structures among bilingual Spanish-speaking students, leading to a proficiency comparable to that of native Spanish-speaking students in a monolingual setting.

PURPOSE OF THE STUDY

The present study investigated and provided descriptive information about the developmental characteristics of twenty-one syntactic and morphological structures present in two written Spanish language samples of native Spanish-speaking students in fourth to ninth grades. The main purposes of this investigation were as follows:

1. To determine measures of consistency between frequency of occurrence of twenty-one variables within two written Spanish language samples (inter-sample reliability), and the reliability of teachers' ratings (inter-rater reliability)

2. To design a reliable and valid procedure in order to derive a predictor equation based on linguistic information that would best indicate

Spanish-speaking students' grade levels and teachers' ratings of the quality of written language samples in a Puerto Rican monolingual setting

3. To apply the predictor equation to written Spanish language samples of native Spanish-speaking students in bilingual education programs to determine whether such characteristics observed in a monolingual Spanish setting could be generalized to a Spanish-English bilingual setting

4. To investigate the degree to which the twenty-one syntactic and morphological variables are associated with the students' grade levels in order to describe developmental patterns of written Spanish.

DEFINITION OF TERMS

- *Adjectivals:* Forms or phrases that function as adjectives.

- *Compound Predicates:* Number of finite verbs joined by a coordinate conjunction or a comma to another verb, and taking the same subject as that verb.

- *Coordinated T-units:* Number of T-units that are not separated by a period or capitalization which indicates a new sentence.

- *Maturity:* As defined by Hunt, "the observed characteristics of writers in an older grade" (Hunt, 1965, p. 20).

- *Sentence Adverbials:* Also known as *sentence introducers* or *sentence signals,* they serve not only to introduce sentences, but also to relate them to previous sentences or situations.

- *Spanish Structural Density:* A qualitative and quantitative analysis of written syntactic and morphological variables in Spanish in order to assess the degree to which these linguistic variables are associated with native Spanish-speaking students' grade levels. The term *structural* is used to allow for the morphological variables as well as the syntactic ones to be included in the investigation.

- *Structure Words:* Adverbs (other than *-mente*), prepositions, determiners, qualifiers, conjunctions, subordinators, and pronouns.

- *Syntactic Density:* Developmental trends in the students' use of certain kinds of linguistic structures are characteristic of increasing maturity (chronological age) and language development. A qualitative and quantitative description of linguistic structures and an analysis of their use make up a factor called *syntactic density* also known as *syntactic complexity,* or *syntactic maturity* (Hunt, 1970; Kidder and Golub, 1976).

- *T-unit:* A "minimal terminal unit," consisting of one main clause plus all subordinate clauses and nonclausal structures attached to or embedded in it (Hunt, 1970).

OVERVIEW OF ANALYSIS OF DATA

Based on the four main objectives of this investigation, the following hypotheses were tested:

Research Objective I: Inter-Sample and Inter-Rater Reliability

Hypothesis 1: There will be a significant positive correlation between the frequency of syntactic and morphological variables within two separate written Spanish language samples by native Spanish-speaking students.

A Pearson-product correlation was calculated for the frequency of occurrence of each of the linguistic variables in two written language samples (total of 200-word sample), to determine the consistency of linguistic indexes. Ten out of twenty-one linguistic variables showed a statistically significant positive correlation ($p < .05$).

Hypothesis 2: There will be a significant positive correlation between the ratings of the written Spanish language samples by different teachers of native Spanish-speaking students.

A Pearson-product correlation was calculated for the ratings between pairs of teachers, and a Spearman Brown prophecy formula was used to estimate the reliability coefficients between raters on a 200-word sample.

Results indicated that correlations between pairs of teachers at each instructional level (fourth to sixth and seventh to ninth grades) were significant ($p < .05$), except for one pair of teachers at each level whose ratings did not correlate significantly.

Research Objective II: Linguistic Variables as Indicators of Students' Grade Levels and Teachers' Ratings in a Monolingual Spanish Setting

Hypothesis 3: There will be a significant correlation between the syntactic and morphological variables and Spanish-speaking students' grade levels in fourth to ninth grades.

A stepwise regression analysis was conducted using each grade level, fourth to ninth grades, as the criterion measure. The sum of the syntactic and morphological structures present in the two Spanish written language samples was used as predictor variables.

Coordinated T-units, sentence adverbials, structure words, compound predicates, and adjectivals were the first five variables to be selected by the multiple regression analysis. The weighted linear combination of these variables made a significant contribution to the prediction of grade levels at fourth to ninth grades—$R(90) = .78$, $p < .01$.

Hypotheses 4 and 5: There will be a significant correlation between the syntactic and morphological variables and teachers' ratings of written Spanish language samples of native Spanish-speaking students in fourth to sixth grades. There will be a significant correlation between the syntactic and morphological variables and teachers' ratings of the written Spanish language samples of native Spanish-speaking students in seventh to ninth grades.

Separate regression analyses were conducted on the fourth- to sixth- and seventh- to ninth-grade compositions. Since independent groups of teachers rated the fourth- to sixth- and seventh- to ninth-grade compositions separately, using a normalized scale of 1-5, one single analysis which would encompass fourth- to ninth-grade language samples was not appropriate. Teachers' ratings (average of two raters) were the criterion measure, and the sum of the frequency of occurrence of each one of the linguistic variables was used as predictor variables. The weighted linear combination of sentence adverbials, structure words, and content words made a significant contribution to the prediction of teachers' ratings at seventh to ninth grades—R (45) = .63, p < .05. In the fourth- to sixth-grade analysis, the number of coordinated T-units significantly correlated with teachers' ratings—R (45) = .47, p < .01—but no additional predictor variables produced a significant increment in the multiple correlation coefficient.

Research Objective III: Linguistic Variables as Indicators of Spanish-Speaking Students' Grade Levels in a Bilingual Setting

Hypothesis 6: There will be a significant correlation between the weighted linear combination of linguistic variables and grade levels of Spanish-speaking students in a bilingual education program.

The Spanish written language samples of Spanish-speaking students in bilingual education programs in Pennsylvania were analyzed, and frequencies of occurrence for each linguistic variable were tabulated. The best equation from the regression analyses conducted on the monolingual Spanish samples was selected to apply to the bilingual sample.

The regression analysis assigned the relative weight to each of the five linguistic variables according to their degree of independent correlation with the criterion measure. Products were obtained by multiplying the frequencies of the variables by their multiple regression weightings, as shown in Table 1. A constant was added to this product, and a score (Spanish Structural Density Score) was obtained for each student. A Pearson-product correlation was calculated between the predicted values thus obtained and students' actual grade levels. The correlation was statistically significant— r (3) = .58, p < .001.

Research Objective IV: Developmental Patterns of Syntactic and Morphological Variables in a Monolingual Setting

Hypothesis 7: There will be a statistically significant correlation between the mean frequency of occurrence of syntactic and morphological

Table 1
A Sample Worksheet for the Computation of Spanish Structural Density Score (SSDS) through the Use of Multiple Regression Weights

Number of each variable obtained from 200-word sample:			Weight:		Product:
Structure Words	_____	X	.04	=	_____
Compound Predicates:	_____	X	.35	=	_____
Coordinated T-units:	_____	X	−.10	=	_____
Sentence Adverbials:	_____	X	.40	=	_____
Adjectivals:	_____	X	.13	=	_____
			Constant	=	2.07
	Total		(SSDS)	=	_____

variables and Spanish-speaking students' grade levels in a monolingual setting.

The mean frequency scores of the twenty-one linguistic variables analyzed in the present study were correlated with students' actual grade level in the monolingual Spanish language samples, in order to describe patterns of development of written syntactic and morphological variables among native Spanish-speaking students. Results are shown in Table 2.

SUMMARY OF THE MAIN FINDINGS

The reliable and valid results obtained in these experiments indicated that Spanish-speaking students' written linguistic development according to grade level can be effectively and efficiently measured. The four main objectives of this investigation were accomplished:

1. The frequency of appearance of some of the linguistic variables in the two samples analyzed was slightly affected by restricted word-sampling, although the overall estimate was statistically significant. Results from the present investigation indicate that a 200-word sample does not yield reliable results for *all* linguistic measures of writing ability.

Overall, the correlations between teachers' ratings were statistically significant ($p < .05$) and moderately high. A median correlation of .72 was obtained for the teachers who rated fourth to sixth graders, and a median correlation of .86 was obtained for the teachers who rated seventh to ninth graders. Subjective differences between the ratings of quality of written

Table 2
Correlations of Linguistic Variable Means with Grade Levels in Fourth to Ninth Grades in Puerto Rican Schools

Number of Variable	Name of Variable	Correlation Coefficient
1	Word Order	−.17
2	Form and Agreement	−.85*
3	Number of Words	−.31
4	Content Words	−.81*
5	Structure Words	.95**
6	Content Words per Structure Words	.90**
7	Verbs of Double and Triple Predicate	.25
8	Compound Predicates	.84*
9	T-units	.89**
10	Coordinated T-units	−.93**
11	Words per T-unit	.74
12	Main and Subordinate Clauses	−.93**
13	Clauses per T-unit	.61
14	Subordinate Clauses	.59
15	Words per Main Clause	.99**
16	Words per Subordinate Clause	.83*
17	Sentence Adverbials	.97**
18	Adverbials	.50
19	Adjectivals	.86*
20	Prepositional Phrases	.54
21	Nominalizations	.08

*$p < .05$
**$p < .01$

Spanish language samples by different teachers made interpretations of the analyses based on teachers' ratings as the criterion measure less generalizable.

2. The formula derived in this investigation to measure written Spanish language development resulted in a valid and reliable measure of linguistic maturity. The stepwise regression analysis assigned relative weightings to the syntactic and morphological variables according to their degree of contribution to the criterion measure, i.e., grade level. A predictor value indicating the students' grade level based on a linear weighted combination of the linguistic variables was derived. Number of coordinated T-units, sentence adverbials, structure words, compound predicates, and adjectivals significantly correlated with students' grade levels, but no additional predictor variables produced a significant increment in the multiple regression

coefficient. Observing the linguistic behavior of these variables, an increase in the number of sentence adverbials, compound predicates, structure words, and adjectivals parallelled an increase in grade levels. Coordinated T-units was the only variable which inversely correlated with grade level, i.e., the higher the grade in which the student was enrolled, the fewer the co-ordinated T-units in the written samples.

3. As a measure of cross-validation, the significant results obtained from the bilingual students' written language samples attested to the validity of the measurement.

Students in the bilingual samples used more coordinated T-units than in the monolingual samples. The decrease in frequency of coordinated T-units was more gradual among Spanish-speaking students in the bilingual education programs than among students in the monolingual Spanish schools. The frequency of occurrence of structure words was higher at the fourth-grade level in the bilingual sample than it was in the monolingual sample, although in higher grades, the number of structure words progressively decreased in the former sample, while it steadily increased in the latter. Increase in frequency of compound predicates, sentence adverbials, and adjectivals was minimal between fourth and sixth grades in the bilingual sample, possibly because these students were placed in the same instructional classroom, based on their reading ability in Spanish or English, regardless of their actual grade level.

4. Written Spanish language development among Spanish-speaking students in Puerto Rico was indicated in this study by an increase in the frequency of sentence adverbials, structure words, compound predicates, adjectivals, words per main and subordinate clauses, words per T-unit, and clauses per T-unit, with a progressive increase in the students' grade levels. The leveling-off point for some of the variables was eighth grade. Determiner form and agreement, content words, ratio of content words per structure words, number of T-units, coordinated T-units, and number of main and subordinate clauses showed an inverse correlation with grade levels. As students progress through school, they seem to use many more recursive embedding rules in order to consolidate sentences and increase the length of the clauses. Earlier grade students combine clauses together by abusing co-ordinating devices.

CONCLUSIONS, APPLICATIONS, AND
IMPLICATIONS FOR FURTHER RESEARCH

Linguistic analysis of written Spanish language development among native Spanish-speaking students has been neglected by language researchers despite the need for this type of information in Spanish-English bilingual education programs in the United States. The present study was a step toward meeting this lack of information, offering a descriptive and qualitative analysis from normative data upon which bilingual education researchers, educators, and language researchers in general can draw pertinent applications. This study was planned mainly to design a reliable and valid procedure for arriving at a linguistic index that would best predict Spanish-speaking students' written linguistic maturity, as well as a practical means to be used for the assessment of language progress.

Norms for this procedure have been established in Puerto Rico and show which are the final significant variables that best indicate a pattern of structural growth and maturity in their native language among Spanish-speaking students. In order to use the derived formula presented in Table 1, and to arrive at a predicted value that will represent the student's level of Spanish structural sophistication (maturity), the following procedure should be observed:

1. Collect two written language samples using different stimulus pictures (200-word sample in all)

2. Count the frequency of occurrence of the five linguistic variables in the two written language samples

3. Multiply the number of occurrence of each variable by its corresponding weighting

4. Add all products plus the constant which determines the Spanish Structural Density Score.

Educators and language testing researchers in bilingual education can use the derived predictor equation formula in order to assess Spanish-speaking students' written linguistic knowledge of their native language, as well as to assess students' progress in their written language throughout the school years. The analysis of the frequency of occurrence of each linguistic variable at each consecutive level in Puerto Rican written samples can serve as baseline data for educators in bilingual education programs. Such an analysis can be used to enrich Spanish-speaking students' written vocabulary and increase the use of the syntactic and morphological structures among bilingual Spanish-speaking students, leading to a proficiency comparable to that of Puerto Rican Spanish-speaking students in Puerto Rico.

Furthermore, since the increase in the use of certain linguistic variables generally drops after grade eight, a continuation of this study up to grade twelve and beyond would discover perhaps new trends of language development as a function of later grades and maturity (chronological age).

Since norms for the development and measurement of various linguistic structures used by Puerto Rican Spanish-speaking children in the writing of their native language have already been established in the present study, it would be possible to further compare groups of students of different Spanish-speaking origin to determine whether significant differences exist among children of different subcultural groups in their capacity to produce written syntactic and morphological structures at different grade levels.

The presence of five significant linguistic structures can be used to assess written linguistic maturity among native Spanish-speaking students. Furthermore, they can be used to test written language development of Anglo American students learning Spanish to see whether there is a similar growth in the Spanish syntax of English-speaking students learning Spanish as a second language.

REFERENCES

Brisk, M.E. "The Spanish Syntax of the Pre-school Spanish-American: The Case of New Mexican Five-year-old Children" (Doctoral dissertation, University of New Mexico, 1972). *Dissertation Abstracts International* 34 (1973): 297-A. (University Microfilms No. 73-16, 585.)

Golub, L.S. *Syntactic Density Score (SDS) with Some Aids for Tabulating.* State College, Pa.: Pennsylvania State University, 1973. ERIC ED 091 741, 1973.

Golub, L.S., and Frederick, W.C. *Linguistic Structures and Deviations in Children's Written Sentences.* Technical report from the Wisconsin Research and Developmental Center for Cognitive Learning, No. 152. Madison, Wisc.: University of Wisconsin, 1970.

_____ . *Linguistic Structures in the Discourse of Fourth and Sixth Graders.* Technical report from the Wisconsin Research and Developmental Center for Cognitive Learning, No. 166. Madison, Wisc.: University of Wisconsin, 1971.

González, G. "The Acquisition of Spanish Grammar by Native Spanish Speakers (Doctoral dissertation, University of Texas at Austin, 1970). *Dissertation Abstracts International* 31, (1971): 6033-A. (University Microfilms No. 71-11, 540.)

Hunt, K.W. *Grammatical Structures Written at Three Grade Levels.* National Council of Teachers of English Research Report No. 3. Champaign, Ill.: NCTE, 1965.

_____ . "Syntactic Maturity in Schoolchildren and Adults." *Monograph of the Society for Research in Child Development* 35, No. 1 (1970): 1-67.

Kernan, K.T., and Blount, B.G. "The Acquisition of Spanish Grammar by Mexican Children." *Anthropological Linguistics* 8 (1966): 1-14.

Kidder, C.L., and Golub, L.S. "Computer Application of a Syntactic Density Measure. "*Computers and the Humanities* 10 (1976): 325-331.

LaBrant, L.L. "A Study of Certain Language Developments of Children in Grades Four to Twelve, Inclusive." *Genetic Psychology Monographs* 14 (1933): 387-491.

Loban, W.D. *The Language of Elementary School Children.* National Council of Teachers of English Report No. 1, Champaign, Ill.: NCTE, 1963.

_____ . *Language Ability Grades Seven, Eight, and Nine.* Cooperative Research Monograph No. 18, U.S. Department of Health, Education and Welfare, Office of Education, 1966.

McCarthy, D. *The Language Development of the Preschool Child.* University of Minnesota Institute of Child Welfare Monograph No. 4. Minneapolis: University of Minnesota Press, 1930.

Templin, M.C. *Certain Language Skills in Children: Their Development and Interrelationships.* Minneapolis: University of Minnesota Press, 1957.

Toronto, A.S. "Developmental Assessment of Spanish Grammar." *Journal of Speech and Hearing Disorders* 41 (1976): 150-171.

The Relationship of Bilingual Bicultural Education and Regular Education in the Verbal and Nonverbal Performances of Chicano Students

Frank Z. Alejandro

Semifinalist, Outstanding Dissertations
National Advisory Council on Bilingual Education

Degree conferred May 1979
Catholic University of America
Washington, D.C.

Dissertation Committee:
John D. Olsen, *Chair*
Leo Y. Min
John J. Convey

About the Author

As Educational Research Specialist with the National Institute of Education
in Washington, D.C., Dr. Frank Z. Alejandro is responsible for developing,
writing regulations for, and implementing the Experimental Program for
Opportunities in Advanced Study and Research in Education, which
emphasizes increased participation by minorities and women in educational
research. Previously, he was national coordinator and personnel management specialist with the Navy Department's Administrative Cooperative
Education Program, where nearly two-thirds of the college graduates he
recruited for career positions were of Hispanic backgrounds. In addition, Dr.
Alejandro has been Executive Director of the National Council for Chicano
Studies, and cofounder of the country's first Chicano college—Colegio
Jacinto Trevino, Centro Educativo Chicano, in south Texas. His many
publications and presentations at national conferences reflect his strong
interest in developing programs of ethnic studies in higher education.

SUMMARY

The purpose of this study was to investigate the relationship of bilingual bicultural education and regular education in students' verbal and nonverbal performances. Specifically, the study sought to determine if there was a significant difference in the verbal and nonverbal performances on the Inter-American Series Test of General Ability (IAS TOGA), English and Spanish subtests, oral vocabulary, numbers, association, and classification, when students in the bilingual bicultural and regular education groups were compared.

The testing of the hypotheses involved sets of Analysis of Variance (ANOVA) using a 2" x 2" factorial design. The F test was used to determine significant differences that were set at the .05 level. The F test revealed that there were significant differences in seven of the sixteen English test comparisons. Eleven of the sixteen Spanish test comparisons were also significant.

One conclusion drawn from these research findings was that Chicano students in the early years of their educational development perform better if they are taught in their dominant language before they are introduced to regular English language instruction. A second conclusion was that as students progress to the upper grades a noticeable improvement is detected in their performance scores. This indicated that as students enrolled in bilingual bicultural education programs progress in their education, they will eventually perform as well as or better than their peers in the regular education program. A third conclusion was that students for the most part perform better on the verbal sections of both the English and Spanish tests.

INTRODUCTION

The major legislative support of bilingual bicultural education in the United States lies in the Bilingual Education Act under Title VII of the Elementary and Secondary Education Act (ESEA) of 1968. The purpose of the act is to develop programs offering a basic competence in English, but to the exclusion of the child's cultural heritage and language. Bilingual bicultural education is a process which allows for the total development of the child by teaching concepts of the history and culture associated with his or her dominant language while he or she is learning to function in another language and culture. Although it is not a new concept, bilingual bicultural education has been reintroduced to U.S. education in an effort to meet the needs of Spanish-speaking and other non-English-speaking students who have limited or no ability to function in English.

BACKGROUND AND STATEMENT
OF THE PROBLEM

The Spanish-speaking population in the United States is estimated roughly at sixteen million. They make up the second largest of our population groups and are known variously as Mexican, Mexican American, Latin,

Latin American, Spanish, Spanish American, Spanish surname, Spanish speaking, Hispanic American, Hispano, Latino, Cubano, Boricua, and Chicano. Of these, approximately ten million are Mexican Americans, most of whom reside in the southwestern part of the United States covering the states of Arizona, California, Colorado, New Mexico, and Texas. Galarza, Gallegos, and Zamora (1970) write that

> In 1960 the highest figure given for the number of persons of Mexican ancestry (Spanish speaking, Spanish surnamed) in five southwestern states was 3.5 million. Today it is estimated to be above five million, and by 1975 the number will be between 5.5 and 6 million. (p. 4)

The Chicano has been the least educated and the most neglected and discriminated citizen in the United States, next to the American Indian (U.S. Commission on Civil Rights, 1974). The Chicano is still far behind the national average in educational attainment. The national median for educational attainment is 12.2 years; for the Spanish-speaking population the median is 9.6, an improvement of two points since the 1960 census statistics were compiled. While the unemployment rate in 1973 was 4.3 for Anglo Americans sixteen years and over, it was 7.5 for the Spanish speaking.

It is suggested that the inability to perform competently in the English language has been a primary factor explaining low educational attainment and high unemployment rates among Chicano youth. In a recently published report on the Spanish speaking, the United States Department of Labor (1973) suggested that the acquisition of a working knowledge of English will open the doors for educational and economic advancement The report states that

> Improvement in English-language skills, [as] both cause and consequence of better educational opportunity, is clearly a major factor in the sharp rise in the educational attainment among the younger people. (p. 94)

The "No Spanish" Rule

The root of the problem stems from the educational system in this country (De León, 1972). As a general policy, the schools in the southwestern part of the United States adopted a "no Spanish" rule which limited and to a great extent otherwise affected the learning capabilities of Mexican American children (U.S. Commission on Civil Rights, 1974). Prior to the 1960s students were punished for speaking Spanish not only in the classroom, but also on any part of the school grounds (National Education Association, 1967). Steiner (1968) reports that in one school in El Paso where the students were taught in Spanish for part of the day, the same children caught talking in Spanish were punished with detention after school. Steiner claims that this practice is still evident in rural schools. Carter (1970), likewise, describes an incident where a teacher in Tucson, Arizona fined children a penny for every word the children spoke in Spanish. The attitude of no Spanish speaking in the school later changed to a policy allowing the use of Spanish at specific times. Basically, if the student did not understand whatever was being explained, it was permissible to speak Spanish in order to clarify certain points as long as one quickly changed to English. Spanish was used as little as possible.

The U.S. Commission on Civil Rights (1974) in its report *Toward Quality Education for Mexican Americans* states that

> Use of Spanish is further discouraged on an unconscious level by school officials. One southwestern educator expressed the view that: "the actual incidence of discouragement is probably much higher than Commission statistics show. Because the schools have for so long felt that Spanish is a handicap to successful learning, they unconsciously foster unacceptance and resulting discouragement of the speaking of Spanish in school." Not only does this practice fail to build on one of the most basic skills of Chicano students, but it degrades them and impedes their education by its implicit refusal to provide for teaching and learning in Spanish. (p. 4)

PURPOSE OF THE STUDY

Meeting the educational needs of students with limited or no English-speaking ability has been a major problem for U.S. schools. It was the purpose of this study to investigate the relationship between bilingual bicultural education and regular education in students' verbal and nonverbal performances. Specifically, the study sought to determine if there was a significant difference in the verbal and nonverbal performances on the InterAmerican Series Test of General Ability, English and Spanish subtests, oral vocabulary, numbers, association, and classification. The study was focused on Chicano students in primary and elementary schools with Title VII funding in the rural southwest region of the United States.

DEFINITION OF TERMS

In order to better understand this research study, it is essential to have a clear knowledge of the terms used throughout. The following definition of terms serves this purpose:

- *Association:* The child's ability to associate one item with its corresponding part; the Spanish Test term is *asociación.*

- *Bilingualism:* The ability to function in another language in addition to the language spoken in one's home.

- *Biculturalism:* The ability to behave on occasions according to selected patterns of a culture other than one's own.

- *Bilingual bicultural education:* An educational process that allows for the total self-development of individuals through the use of their home language and culture while they are learning to function in the second language and culture.

- *Chicano (Mexican American):* An American of Mexican descent. Among the younger generations the term *Chicano* has been popularized. Government publications and other literary works use the words *Chicano* and *Mexican American* interchangeably. In this study the term is used interchangeably with *Spanish speaking.*

- *Classification:* The child's understanding and knowledge of words expressed nonverbally; the Spanish Test term is *clasificación.*

- *Dominant language:* The language that the child brings from the home. In this study the dominant language is Spanish.

- *Inter-American Series Test of General Ability:* The series is made up of subtests that measure verbal-numerical (verbal) and nonverbal performances. It comprises an English and a Spanish version.

- *Oral vocabulary:* The students' understanding and knowledge of words expressed verbally; the Spanish Test term is *vocabulario oral.*

- *Regular education:* Traditional classroom instruction in English.

- *Spanish-speaking American:* A generic term used to refer to the following cultural groups: Chicanos, Puerto Ricans, Cubans, Latins, and other Hispanics.

BILINGUAL BICULTURAL EDUCATION: INSTRUCTION IN THE DOMINANT LANGUAGE
A Theoretical Framework

Language communication has always been a problem between the Mexican American people and their Anglo American peers. Large numbers of the Spanish-speaking community who have been in the United States for many years have not learned to speak, read, or write in English. The Department of Labor (1973) in its report on the Spanish speaking states that

> Inability to speak English becomes a major problem for children as early as elementary school. Everywhere in the past, and even now in many places, no special help has been provided for Spanish-speaking youngsters entering school, though without such help they are likely to develop learning problems and . . . subsequent high dropout rates. The seriousness of the problem is illustrated by the situation, in some southwestern school districts, where about 40 percent of the children of Mexican American origin have in the recent past been placed in classes for the slow learners and the mentally retarded. (p. 108)

Recently, some educators have agreed that the best medium for teaching the child, particularly during the early stages of learning, is through dominant language instruction (Andersson and Boyer, 1970). Valencia (1972) writes:

> The current movement in bilingual education points up four underlying principles: use of the learner's native language to facilitate the learning process and avoid postponement of cognitive and psychomotor development; maintenance and perpetuation of the child's first language, along with other cultural aspects; recognition of the child's ethnicity as acceptable and noteworthy and recognition of the desirability of bilingualism. (p. 1)

Armando Rodríguez (1968) in addressing the National Conference on Educational Opportunities for Mexican Americans stated:

> Bilingual education is critical for hundreds of thousands of youngsters. Language is not just an instrument for communication and learning; it is a set of values. It is his being. It is a door that we can open so the youngster can see and live and be a part of two cultures—two societies. (p. 21)

The Advisory Committee for the Education of the Spanish Speaking and Mexican Americans (1973) recommended

> That programs in bilingual bicultural education in both Spanish and English be established in every school whose Spanish-speaking membership is 20 percent or higher, of its total school enrollment. Minimally, in those schools where there is a sufficient number of Spanish-speaking students at any level to warrant group instruction in basic skills, instruction in Spanish language arts and culture must be provided, along with English as a second language. Optimally, a progam in bilingual bicultural education should be designed for both Spanish-speaking children and native English-speaking children and include instruction in both Spanish and English in all curriculum areas. (pp. 20-21)

RESEARCH HYPOTHESES

The specific research hypotheses investigated and analyzed for both English and Spanish tests are as follows:

Hypothesis 1. There will be no significant difference in the verbal performance, as measured by the *Inter-American Series Tests of General Ability Subtest, Oral Vocabulary*, between students in the bilingual bicultural education group and students in the regular education group.

Hypothesis 2. There will be no significant difference in the verbal performance, as measured by the *Inter-American Series Tests of General Ability Subtest, Numbers*, between students in the bilingual bicultural education group and students in the regular education group.

Hypothesis 3. There will be no significant difference in the nonverbal performance, as measured by the *Inter-American Series Tests of General Ability*

Subtest, Association, between students in the bilingual bicultural education group and students in the regular education group.

Hypothesis 4. There will be no significant difference in the nonverbal performance, as measured by the *Inter-American Series Tests of General Ability Subtest, Classification,* between students in the bilingual bicultural education group and students in the regular education group.

OVERVIEW OF ANALYSES OF DATA

The analysis of variance (ANOVA) technique was selected to treat the data in this research study. ANOVA was used because it is a strong parametric statistic concerned with the variance as a measure of variability. It assumes "that the samples with which we work have been drawn from populations that are normally distributed" (Kerlinger, 1973, p. 286). ANOVA further assumes that the samples are randomly selected and that the variance within these samples is statistically the same. Kerlinger (1973) refers to this assumption as homogeneity of variance.

The F-test was used to determine the significance of the differences between the means. The level of confidence for determining significance was set at the .05 level. An F-ratio was computed for each compared group to determine whether the variance of the groups differed. An F-ratio found to be significant at the .05 indicated that the difference obtained between the groups compared was true and not caused by chance. The between-groups variance was used in determining the value of F.

An entry performance test was administered in September 1973 to both groups, treatment and comparative. Both Spanish and English forms of the IAS were used for this purpose. Pupils in kindergarten were given the pre-school level of the IAS, Spanish and English forms. Pupils in grade 1 were given Level One of the IAS, Spanish and English forms. Pupils in grades 2 and 3 were given Level Two of the IAS, Spanish and English forms. A posttest was administered in May 1974. The pre- and posttest scores for each student were recorded on Fortran coding sheets. Demographic data were also collected for each student and recorded on individual student registration forms. Students who did not have complete pre- and posttest data were excluded from the analyses.

The unit of analysis was the student (n=1,383). Each student was assigned an identification number. For purposes of statistical analysis, students in bilingual bicultural education (independent variable) were arbitrarily given a number code of *1;* students in regular education (independent variable) were assigned a number code of *2.* Males were *1;* females were *2.* The students' grade level was also assigned a number code as follows: *4* for kindergarten, *1* for grade 1, *2* for grade 2, and *3* for grade 3.

In order to facilitate these analyses, pre- and posttests means and standard deviations for each of the criterion variables were obtained by group and by sex for each grade. The criterion variables were the students' verbal and nonverbal performance scores on the English Test (oral vocabulary, numbers, association, and classification), and verbal and nonverbal performance scores on the Spanish Test (*vocabulario oral, números, asociación,* and *clasificación*).

FINDINGS

The general findings of this study support providing bilingual bicultural education for Chicano students in grades kindergarten through 3 in that the performances of the bilingual group were shown to be significantly higher than the performances of the comparative group in most of the criterion measures analyzed. While there were only two instances where the regular education group students outperformed the bilingual group students, there were sixteen instances where opposite results were found. In short, of the sixteen hypotheses tested on the English Test only seven were rejected. Interestingly, the Spanish Test results rejected eleven of the sixteen hypotheses tested.

CONCLUSIONS

The following conclusions are derived from the analyses performed on each criterion variable for students in each group for each grade, and the related discussion on the findings reported by analysis of variance on the English and Spanish subtests:

1. Chicano students in the early years of their educational development perform better on standardized tests of general ability if they are taught initially in their dominant language before they are introduced to regular English language instruction.

2. As students progress to the upper grades a noticeable improvement is detected in their subtest performance scores. This indicates that as students enrolled in bilingual bicultural education programs progress in their education, they will eventually perform at the same level as or better than their peers in the regular education program.

3. Chicano students for the most part perform better on the verbal sections of both the English and Spanish Tests, but their overall performance is better on the Spanish Test.

RECOMMENDATIONS

The majority of the research done and the conclusions reached by investigations of this kind have been inconclusive because of the continuous use of existing, ongoing bilingual bicultural programs that are considered pilot activities or otherwise experimental in nature. The conclusions presented earlier will, it is hoped, add some light to this condition. The following are offered as recommendations:

1. A followup study for grades kindergarten through 3 using Spanish-speaking and, perhaps, English-speaking students at a different geographical area should be initiated.

2. A study that will investigate the effects of bilingual bicultural education in grades kindergarten through 3 on other variables such as reading, social studies, mathematics, and self-concept should be conducted.

3. A research effort with a primary focus on the validity and reliability of the Inter-American Tests of General Ability and the Pruebas de Habilidad General, with primary, elementary, and secondary school populations of the different Spanish-speaking subgroups in the different parts of the United States, should be supported.

4. Investment of additional resources by the United States Office of Education and the National Institute of Education to develop, implement, coordinate, and disseminate materials and research data of ongoing, exemplary programs should be supported.

5. It is recommended that the Office of Bilingual Education, United States Office of Education, and the National Institute of Education launch a national effort in cooperation with local, state, and other federal and private agencies to research thoroughly the area of bilingual bicultural education. This could provide an abundance of needed data on similarities and dissimilarities of programs now in operation.

6. It is recommended that these agencies conduct analyses of the different teaching methods presently used throughout the country, especially in ESEA Title VII programs, to determine the relative effect these programs have on pupil performance, verbal and nonverbal.

7. It is imperative that researchers look closely at the results produced by teaching children entirely in their native language, teaching English as a second language, using dominant language instruction for extended periods, alternating English and the dominant language continuously or in sequence, and using the dominant language for one learning area and English for another.

8. It is recommended that a comprehensive study of a descriptive nature be launched to investigate all bilingual bicultural education programs nationwide. Such a study should provide empirical data on analyses performed in relation to program components: instruction, development and dissemination of materials, testing and evaluation of instruments, staff development, management and community participation and involvement, and program cost effectiveness. It is hoped that such data could reveal the nature and magnitude of the underlying differences between successful and unsuccessful bilingual bicultural education programs.

APPENDIX

Point of Clarification

It is important to note that the research study submitted was completed in fall 1976. It should be read in that context. The Dissertation Committee did not accept the study until February 1979. A successful defense of the dissertation was held 23 April 1979 and the Ph.D. degree was awarded 12 May 1979.

Population and Sample

Specific conditions were used in the selection of the population. This investigator was interested in studying the relationship between bilingual bicultural education and regular education in the verbal and nonverbal performances of Chicano students in grades kindergarten through 3. In order to do this, specific conditions for the identification of projects that offered these kinds of instruction had to be established. The following conditions were used in identifying this population:

1. Projects had to be funded under the ESEA of 1965 as amended.

2. Projects had to be classified as Title VII and funded under the Bilingual Education Act of 1968.

3. Projects had to be part of a primary or elementary school offering bilingual bicultural education and regular education in grades kindergarten through 3 as part of the curriculum offerings.

4. Projects were required to have Spanish as the dominant language of instruction and to be serving Mexican American students primarily.

5. Projects had to be located in a rural area with a population of 30,000 or less in the southwest region of the United States.

Twelve projects which met these conditions for the 1974 fiscal year were identified. A sample of 25 percent of these twelve projects was selected at random. The sample consisted of these three projects serving 1,383 students in grades kindergarten through 3.

REFERENCES

Advisory Committee for the Education of the Spanish Speaking and Mexican Americans. *A Challenge to Reality—El Desafío a La Realidad.* Annual Report to the Secretary of DHEW. 1 May 1973, pp. 20-21.

Andersson, T., and Boyer, M. *Bilingual Schooling in the United States* (2 vols.). Washington, D.C.: U.S. Government Printing Office, 1970.

Carter, T.P. *Mexican Americans in School: A History of Educational Neglect.* New York: College Entrance Examinations Board, 1970.

De León, N. *Chicanos: Our Background and Our Pride.* Lubbock, Tex.: Trucha Publications, 1972.

Galarza, E.; Gallegos, H.; and Zamora, J. *Mexican Americans in the Southwest.* Santa Barbara, Calif.: McNally and Loftin, 1970.

Kerlinger, F.N. *Foundations of Behavioral Research.* New York: Holt, Rinehart and Winston, 1973.

National Education Association. *The Invisible Minority: A Report of the NEA-Tucson Survey on the Teaching of Spanish to the Spanish-Speaking.* Washington, D.C.: National Education Association, 1966.

Rodríguez, A. "Bilingual Education." *National Conference of Educational Opportunities for Mexican Americans.* Austin, Tex.: Southwest Educational Development Laboratory, 25-26 April 1968.

Steiner, S. *La Raza: The Mexican Americans.* New York: Harper and Row, 1968.

U.S., Commission on Civil Rights. *Toward Quality Education for Mexican Americans.* Washington, D.C.: U.S. Government Printing Office, 1974.

U.S., Department of Labor. *Spanish-Speaking Americans: Their Manpower Problems and Opportunities.* A reprint from the 1973 Manpower Report of the President. Washington, D.C.: U.S. Government Printing Office, 1973.

Valencia, A.A. *Bilingual-Bicultural Education for the Spanish-English Bilingual.* Las Vegas, N.M.: New Mexico Highlands University Press, 1972.

A Psycholinguistic Analysis of the Oral Reading Miscues of Selected Field-Dependent and Field-Independent Native Spanish-speaking, Mexican American First Grade Children

Arlinda Jane Eaton

Semifinalist, Outstanding Dissertations
National Advisory Council on Bilingual Education

Degree conferred August 1979
University of Texas at Austin
Austin, Texas

Dissertation Committee:
Thomas D. Horn, *Co-chair*
Rudolph F. Martin, *Co-chair*
George M. Blanco
Frank J. Guszak
Betty J. Mace-Matluck

About the Author

Currently Assistant Professor in Elementary Education at California State University, Northridge, Dr. Arlinda J. Eaton has focused on diagnosing reading difficulties and facilitating reading progress among bilingual students. She has conducted university courses on elementary school reading education and bilingual teaching strategies, and elementary through high school courses on English, Spanish, and language arts. Her publications and presentations include analyses of the effects of learner characteristics and type of instruction on reading achievement, development of diagnostic-prescriptive reading programs, and workshops on teaching reading to bilingual students.

SUMMARY

The present study was designed to analyze in depth and describe the oral reading behavior of native Spanish-speaking Mexican American children who were identified by the *Children's Embedded Figures Test* (Witkin, 1950) as being field dependent (FD), field dependent/independent (FD/I), and field independent (FI) in cognitive style orientation, as they read in their native language, Spanish, and in their second language, English.

Major findings include the following:

1. FD and FI groups looked like distinct groups when they read in both languages.

2. Reading strategies employed did not vary according to the language in which subjects read; there was one reading process.

3. All subjects drew on the same linguistic cue systems while reading in both languages. Generally, FIs employed cue systems to a greater extent than did FDs.

4. FIs comprehended more during the reading act than did FDs in both languages.

5. FIs retold a greater amount of their reading than did FDs. Both related more in Spanish than in English.

STATEMENT OF THE PROBLEM

The purpose of this exploratory study was to investigate individual cognitive processes, or styles, as they related to the oral reading strategies employed by native Spanish-speaking Mexican American, first grade children as they read in both English and Spanish. The design of the study called for an understanding of the oral reading strategies as revealed by an indepth analysis of readers' miscues in their two languages. The Reading Miscue Inventory (Y. Goodman and Burke, 1972) allowed the researcher to analyze miscues at different levels of linguistic organization in order to describe the ongoing processing.

Issuing from the problem statement were three general questions:

1. Does cognitive style, in particular field dependence/independence, influence an individual's orientation toward processing written language?

2. Do the reading strategies employed by a bilingual individual vary according to the language in which he or she reads?

3. Is there more than one reading process?

The following specific research questions were developed from these general questions:

Do bilingual readers identified and grouped as FDs, FD/Is, and FIs (Appendix A) reading in Spanish and English—

1. Employ the same linguistic strategies in their attempt to reconstruct meaning from print?

2. Employ linguistic strategies *to the same extent* in their attempt to reconstruct meaning from print?

3. Comprehend equally well while reading?

4. Verbally express an equal understanding of the material after they have read?

5. Produce miscues which involve:
   a. dialect
   b. intonation
   c. graphic similarity
   d. sound similarity
   e. grammatical function
   f. correction
   g. grammatical acceptability
   h. semantic acceptability
   i. meaning change?

The study, then, was basically descriptive, its goal being to describe linguistically, as detailed in the Reading Miscue Inventory (RMI), what behaviors bilingual FD, FD/I, and FI children demonstrate when they read orally.

PURPOSE OF THE STUDY

Readers are active participants in the reading act; they are not passive reactors merely repeating the author's words found on the page (K. Goodman, 1965). Consequently, readers' thoughts and language cue not only their expected responses (printed words), but also their observed responses (deviations from printed words). This phenomenon leads one to believe that readers' miscues, or deviations from print, are not random (Burke and K. Goodman, 1970). They use the interrelated cue systems of language— graphophonic, syntactic, and semantic—in conjunction with their conceptual and experiential background to reconstruct meaning from print. The ways in which readers employ these cue systems may be referred to as their linguistic strategies.

When individuals approach a reading task, they are confronted with a situation of response uncertainty (F. Smith, 1973; 1978). As a means of reducing this uncertainty, the readers impose their own organization upon the task. They select only what they need from the cue systems in order to reconstruct meaning from the print. Their selection is influenced necessarily by their own established patterns of coping with environmental stimuli.

Cognitive style patterns, in particular field dependence/independence, then, may well influence the types of cues that readers select in order to reconstruct meaning and to impose organization onto the reading task, as well as the extent to which they use those particular cues.

The significance of this study can be viewed from several perspectives. First, to the researcher's knowledge, of all the studies that have attempted to relate reading and cognitive style, only two investigations (Davey, 1971; Readence, 1975) have looked at reading as a language process. Davey discussed the cognitive style construct based upon the work of Kagan, which refers to the manner in which an individual perceptually and conceptually organizes and categorizes visual stimuli as analytic/nonanalytic. Readence, on the other hand, studied the impulsivity/reflectivity dimension of cognitive style. Therefore, the present study offered an original approach in the sense that it involved the FD/I dimension as it relates to the reading process.

Second, this investigation looked at *process* rather than *product*, in contrast to the large majority of recent studies within this area. As Goodenough (Stone, 1976) has reported, cognitive style affects *how* one processes, not *how much*. Consequently, those studies that correlated cognitive style and reading achievement (Santostefano et al., 1965; Stuart, 1967; Watson, 1969; Kaplan, 1969; Annesley, 1971; Wineman, 1971) are viewed with reservations by this researcher. Too, the need to study interactions between linguistic parameters and individual cognitive differences has been emphasized and cited in the literature (Ohnmacht, 1970). Cognitive style research may offer useful understandings of reading underachievement.

Last, never before have bilingual children alone formed the sample in any of the investigations attempting to view reading as a process related to cognitive style. Furthermore, no perceptual-style sample population has ever read in two languages, as did the subjects of this study.

Therefore, the researcher considered the study substantially significant and intended for it to (1) add supportive data from a bilingual perspective to the body of reading miscue research; (2) prove useful to those engaged in research of the reading process; (3) provide useful information to educators and those responsible for curriculum planning for bilingual students; (4) contribute to the growing understanding of the interrelationships of reading as a language process with cognitive strategies; (5) add data to the most extensively studied cognitive style—field dependence/independence; and (6) generate new hypotheses concerning the reading process and the construct of field dependence/independence.

DEFINITION OF TERMS

- *Native tongue,* frequently used synonymously with *mother tongue, first language,* or *dominant language,* is that language acquired first by a child and used as a medium of communication. In this study, however, *dominant language* was not used interchangeably with *native tongue, mother tongue,* or *first language.* There are a number of cases in which individuals' native language is no longer their dominant language.

- *Miscue* refers to any response generated by the subject during oral reading that does not correspond to the graphic display in the text.

- *Cognitive style,* as regarded in this study, is a characteristic mode of mental functioning. Each individual has preferred and self-consistent ways of processing information, of organizing what is heard, seen, remembered, or thought about. Cognitive style is viewed as a stable trait or a pervasive disposition in the individual.

- *Field-dependent* (FD) individuals are those whose perception is strongly dominated by the overall organization of the prevailing field. Their global quality of perception is characterized by a relative inability to perceive parts of a field as being discrete units.

- *Field-independent* (FI) individuals are those who experience items as more or less separate from the surrounding field, rather than fused with it.

- *Field-dependent/independent* (FD/I) individuals are those whose perception is neither predominantly field dependent nor field independent; that is, the individuals would fall somewhere between the two extremes of the continuum.

THEORETICAL FRAMEWORK

Psycholinguistic Theory and Reading

Psycholinguistics is the study of the interrelationships of thought and language. K. Goodman (1976b) has coined the term to express his view of reading: namely, reading is a "psycholinguistic guessing game." An understanding of such a view of the reading process must depend on an understanding of how language works as well as an understanding of how language is used. Reading, as of late, is seen as part of a process of communication (F. Smith, 1973, 1978; Ruddell, 1976).

Working on the assumption that reading is a language process, K. Goodman and his associates listened to children read aloud so that they might analyze their oral reading miscues. The children not only supported the validity of Goodman's assumption, but also generated numerous miscues which in turn served as the base for the development of a theory and model of the reading process (K. Goodman and Y. Goodman, 1977).

The basic premises that underlie a psycholinguistic view of the reading process (K. Goodman, 1976c) include the following:

1. *Reading is language.* It is one of the two active/receptive language processes. Whether one is reading or listening, the goal remains the same: comprehension of meaning.

2. *Readers are users of language.* That is, they use language to obtain meaning. Acceptance of this view leads to another: literacy becomes an extension of a learner's natural language development (K. Goodman, 1972a). Written language, therefore, is not secondary to oral language but rather is an alternate, parallel form of language for literate language users (K. Goodman, 1970).

3. *Language is the means by which people communicate with each other.* The written form of language makes communication possible over space and time.

Reading, then, as defined by K. Goodman (1976a, p. 472), ". . . is a complex process by which a reader reconstructs, to some degree, a message encoded by a writer in graphic language." This definition makes readers active participants; they interact with written language (K. Goodman, 1965). Their reading behavior is cued or miscued during this interaction primarily by four different cue systems operating simultaneously. These cues appear (1) within words—letter-sound relationships, configurations, known little words within bigger words, and recurrent spelling patterns; (2) in the flow of language—patterns of words, inflections, function words, intonation, and referential meaning of prior and subsequent language elements and whole utterances; (3) external to language and reader—pictures, prompting by others, concrete objects, and skills charts; and (4) within the reader—language facility, experiential background, conceptual background, reading attack skills, and learning strategies acquired or taught. Any combination of these cues may be used by readers to reconstruct a message encoded by a writer in graphic language.

The extent to which readers can get meaning from written language depends on how much related meaning they bring to it (K. Goodman, 1977). Thus, in reading, meaning is both input and output (K. Goodman, 1972b). As stated by Smith:

> Reading is less a matter of extracting sound from print than of bringing meaning to print. The sounds that are supposed to reveal the meaning of sequences of letters cannot in fact be produced unless a probable meaning can be determined in advance. (Smith, 1978, p. 2)

It has proven to be far easier to read something for which the reader has a strong conceptual background. Smith (1978) discusses this issue in terms of visual and nonvisual information. The information on the printed page that gets through the eyes to the brain can be referred to as visual information. Nonvisual information, on the other hand, is the information already behind the eyeballs, so to speak, not information one expects to find on the page. Knowledge of the relevant language, of the subject matter, and of how to read are all essential for reading and may be classified as nonvisual information. A reciprocal relationship exists between visual and nonvisual information. That is, the more nonvisual information readers have, the less visual information they need. This relationship exists because the non-visual information lessens the readers' uncertainty in advance and reduces the amount of visual information required to eliminate remaining uncertainty. Smith contends that ". . . what transpires behind the reader's eyes, in the reader's brain, makes a far greater contribution to reading than the print in front of the reader's face" (1978, p. 4).

Nature of Field Dependence/Field Independence

The term *cognitive style* has appeared in the psychological literature since the turn of the century, with considerable contributions made by German psychologists. It has been defined in various ways, as noted in Appendix B.

To explain the nature of the field-dependence/independence dimension, a historical approach is taken to describe with accuracy the evolution of this dimension (Witkin, et al., 1977). In his earliest work, Witkin was concerned with how people locate the upright position in space. He learned that individuals make reference not only to the sensations from within their bodies, but also to the visual environment around them. His subsequent experiment dealt with separating the visual and bodily standards in order to determine their roles in the perception of the upright.

In the *Rod and Frame Test* (RFT) the visual framework is a luminous square frame which is presented to an individual in a completely darkened room. Both the luminous frame and its rod can be rotated at their center, clockwise or counterclockwise, independently of each other. As the frame and rod are presented to an individual in various tilted positions, the task becomes that of adjusting the rod to a position where it is perceived as upright, while the frame around it remains in its initial position of tilt.

Witkin noted marked individual differences among people in how they performed this task. There were those who, in order for the rod to be perceived as properly upright, found it necessary to fully align the rod with its surrounding frame, whatever the position of the frame. On the other hand, there were those individuals who, in making the rod straight, adjusted it more or less close to the upright regardless of the position of the surrounding frame. In other words, they perceived the rod as an entity discrete from the prevailing visual frame and determined the uprightness of the rod according to the felt position of the body, not according to the visual frame immediately surrounding it. Another important observation regarding performance on this test was that the majority of people fell somewhere in between these two extremes; performance was characterized as continuous.

Rather than have an external object (rod) serve as the object of perception, Witkin decided to devise another test in which the individual's body itself would serve as the object of perception. In the *Body Adjustment Test* (BAT) the individual is required to sit in a chair, one that can be tilted clockwise or counterclockwise, which is then projected into a small room that can also be tilted clockwise or counterclockwise, independently of the chair. Once the chair and room are brought to specified tilted settings, the individual is requested to adjust the chair to a position where it is experienced as upright.

A third test, similar to the two previous ones in its essential perceptual structure, even though it did not involve the perception of the upright or the body, was the *Embedded Figures Test* (EFT). This task involved showing an individual a simple figure for a designated period of time. After the simple figure was removed from the individual's sight, a complex figure was shown to the individual who was then directed to locate the simple figure within it.

Witkin found that all three tests provided a quantitative indicator of the extent to which the surrounding organized field had influenced an individual's perception of an item within it: (1) the amount of tilt of the rod or body, in degrees, once the items were reported to be straight; and (2) the amount of time required to locate the simple figure within the complex design. Furthermore, self-consistency in performance across the three tasks was apparent. That is, the people who tilted the rod far toward the tilted frame in making it straight were the same ones who tilted their body far toward the tilted room to perceive the body as upright, as well as the ones who took a long time to locate the simple figure within a complex design.

The common factor underlying the individual differences in performance on the three measures is the extent to which a person perceives analytically and overcomes an embedding context. Witkin employed the terms *field dependence* and *field independence* to explain this phenomenon. Field dependence refers to the mode of perception at one extreme of the performance range, where the prevailing field strongly dominates perception. At the other extreme of the performance range lies the mode of perception referred to as field independence, where items are experienced as more or less separate from the surrounding field. Moreover, scores from all three of these measures of field dependence/independence form a continuous distribution, which indicates that classifications merely reflect a tendency, in varying degrees of strength, toward one mode of perception or the other. There is clearly no implication that two distinct types of people exist.

OVERVIEW OF ANALYSES OF DATA

The task of analyzing the data began after all audiotaping of the readings by the subjects had been completed. The researcher listened to tapes of the oral readings as many times as was necessary to ensure that all deviations from the text could be precisely identified as well as added to the duplicated copies which were initially marked at the time of the reading sessions. Each tape was heard at least three times.

The second step in the analysis involved the coding of those deviations which were counted and included as miscues in the study. Inclusion or exclusion of miscues was determined by the guidelines set forth in the RMI (Y. Goodman and Burke, 1972).

The RMI required decisions in nine categories for each miscue produced. The questions used by the researcher to facilitate the classification of miscues follow:

1. *Dialect*—Is a dialect variation involved in the miscue?

2. *Intonation*—Is a shift in intonation involved in the miscue?

3. *Graphic similarity*—How much does the miscue look like that which was expected?

4. *Sound similarity*—How much does the miscue sound like that which was expected?

5. *Grammatical function*—Is the grammatical function of the miscue the same as the grammatical function of the word in the text?

6. *Correction*—Is the miscue corrected?

7. *Grammatical acceptability*—Does the miscue occur in a structure which is grammatically acceptable?

8. *Semantic acceptability*—Does the miscue occur in a structure which is semantically acceptable?

9. *Meaning change*—Does the miscue result in a change of meaning?

Comprehension and grammatical relationships were also included in the total analysis.

As each of the subject's twenty-five miscues was considered in each of the above categories, the researcher recorded the answers by marking the appropriate subcategories for each item on the Reading Miscue Inventory Coding Sheet. Descriptive statistics obtained in each language for individuals and groups, identified by cognitive style orientation, consisted of percentage frequencies and means.

The statistical analysis of the RMI includes a retelling score which measures the reader's understanding of that which has already been read. According to the RMI, this score is obtained by adding points designated to show the reader's awareness of character analysis, theme, plot, and events. However, after personally communicating with Y. Goodman (1978), the investigator obtained retelling scores in the same manner as the Goodmans' most recent research—the 100 retelling points were divided between character analysis and events; plot and theme were noted even though points were not assigned to them. Seldom have researchers themselves been able to agree on plot and theme.

Each story was analyzed in advance of the taping and numerical points were assigned to each category so that, as the readers expressed their understanding of the selections, they accumulated points as their retellings corresponded to the precalculated analyses. Retelling scores were integrated with the statistical data derived from the coding sheets for interpretation.

A comparative profile for each subject was compiled which summarizes all statistical findings in each language. Group comparisons in each of the nine categories of the RMI have been depicted in tables and frequency distributions.

MAIN FINDINGS AND TENTATIVE CONCLUSIONS

1. Native Spanish-speaking Mexican American bilingual readers, identified and grouped as FD and FI in cognitive style orientation, looked like distinct groups when they read in both Spanish and English. The manner in which they processed printed material looked very much the same across languages. For the most part, the FIs employed the various cue systems to a greater extent than did the FDs.

2. The reading strategies employed by the bilingual subjects of the present analysis did not vary according to the language in which they read; the same strategies were applied across languages. These data support previous research findings which also indicate that there is one reading process.

3. All subjects drew on the same linguistic cue systems in their attempts to reconstruct meaning from print while reading in both their first and second languages. The difference between the two extreme groups lies in the extent to which they employed the cue systems.

4. The FI readers comprehended more during the reading act than did the FDs in both Spanish and English. The FIs appeared to understand substantially more while reading in their first language, whereas the FDs understood slightly more while reading in their second language.

5. Retelling figures paralleled each other across languages; the FIs retold a greater amount of their reading than did the FDs. Both were able to relate a considerably greater amount of their reading in Spanish than of their reading in English.

IMPLICATIONS

The research findings set forth in this dissertation provide certain implications for instructional programs, as noted below:

1. The FI readers processed printed material in both Spanish and English in a manner distinct from those readers identified as FD by the *Children's Embedded Figures Test* (Witkin, 1950). Whatever the differences in cognitive style strategies, once FI and FD cognitive style strategies have been ascertained, practice with their less developed strategies should be provided for *both* groups.

2. Both the FI and FD groups read with more gain in meaning in Spanish, a fact which seems to corroborate the notion that better oral control of a

language provides better results *in the beginning stages* of the reading process.

3. Since reading strategies were shown to be the same across languages, these strategies need not be retaught when reading instruction commences in the other language.

APPENDIX A

The subjects were identified as FD, FD/I, and FI by the *Children's Embedded Figures Test* (CEFT). The CEFT, developed by Witkin (1950), is a version of the *Embedded Figures Test* (EFT) adapted for younger children. Designed after the Gottschaldt figures, Witkin's task is one in which the child is shown a simple geometric figure which is then removed while a complex drawing is presented. This drawing, which contains a figure identical to the simple one, constitutes the embedding context. Unlike the adult version of the test, the simple figure is embedded in a meaningful context rather than in an abstract design. The subject must identify and outline this simple figure in the drawing.

The CEFT provided scores that formed a continuous distribution ranging from 4 to 15. A median split was performed on these scores. The median for the eighteen subjects was 10.5. The ten subjects whose scores fell within one standard deviation from the mean, 9.8, were classified as FD/I because their scores indicated that their perception was neither predominantly FD nor predominantly FI. Those subjects with scores that extended beyond one standard of deviation from the mean were considered FIs; the latter numbered three in this sample. Those with scores that extended beyond a negative one standard of deviation from the mean were five in number. For the purposes of this study, these five were classified as FDs.

APPENDIX B

The term *cognitive style* has been defined as follows:

> . . . a psychological construct that abstractly represents a domain of observable behaviors . . . used most frequently to denote consistencies in individual modes of functioning in a variety of behavioral situations. (Coop and Sigel, 1971, p. 152)

> . . . a term that refers to stable individual preferences in mode of perceptual organization and conceptual categorization of the external environment . . . . (Kagan, Moss, and Sigel, 1973, p. 74)

> Cognitive styles can be most directly defined as individual variation in modes of perceiving, remembering, and thinking, or as distinctive ways of apprehending, storing, transforming, and utilizing information. It may be noted that abilities also involve the foregoing properties, but a difference in emphasis should be noted: Abilities concern level of skill—the more and less of performance—whereas cognitive styles give greater weight to the manner and form of cognition. (Kogan, 1971, p. 244)

> First, cognitive styles are concerned with the form rather than the content of cognitive activity. They refer to individual differences in how we perceive, think, solve problems, learn, relate to others, etc. The definition of cognitive styles is thus cast in process terms. . . . Second, cognitive styles are pervasive dimensions. They cut across the boundaries traditionally—and, we believe, inappropriately—used in compartmentalizing the human psyche and so help restore the psyche to its proper status as a holistic entity. . . . A third characteristic of cognitive styles is that they are stable over time. This does not imply that they are unchangeable. . . . Fourth, with regard to value judgments, cognitive styles are bipolar. This characteristic is of particular importance in distinguishing cognitive styles from intelligence and other ability dimensions . . . each pole has adaptive value under specified circumstances, and so may be judged positively in relation to those circumstances. (Witkin et al., 1977, pp. 15-16)

REFERENCES

Annesley, F.R. *Cognitive Style as a Variable in the Reading Achievement and Intelligence of Boys.* Unpublished doctoral dissertation, Temple University, 1971.

Burke, C.L., and Goodman, K.S. "When a Child Reads: A Psycholinguistic Analysis." *Elementary English* 47 (1970): 121-129.

Coop, R.H., and Sigel, I.E. "Cognitive Style: Implications for Learning and Instruction." *Psychology in the Schools* 8 (1971): 152-161.

Davey, B. *A Psycholinguistic Investigation of Cognitive Style and Oral Reading Strategies in Achieving and Underachieving Fourth Grade Boys.* Unpublished doctoral dissertation, Case Western Reserve University, 1971.

Goodman, K.S. "A Linguistic Study of Cues and Miscues in Reading." *Elementary English* (1965): 639-643.

_____ . "Psycholinguistic Universals in the Reading Process." *Journal of Typographic Research* (1970): 103-110.

_____ . "Reading: The Key is in Children's Language." *Reading Teacher* (1972a): 505-508.

_____ . "The Reading Process: Theory and Practice." In *Language and Learning to Read: What Teachers Should Know About Language,* edited by R.E. Hodges and E.H. Rudorf. Boston, Mass.: Houghton Mifflin Company, 1972b.

_____ . "Behind the Eye: What Happens in Reading." In *Theoretical Models and Processes of Reading,* edited by H. Singer and R.B. Ruddell. Newark, Del.: International Reading Association, 1976a, pp. 470-496.

_____ . "Reading: A Psycholinguistic Guessing Game." In *Theoretical Models And Processes of Reading,* edited by H. Singer and R.B. Ruddell. Newark Del.: International Reading Association, 1976b pp. 497-508.

_____ . "What We Know about Reading." In *Findings of Research in Miscue Analysis: Classroom Implications,* edited by P.D. Allen and D.J. Watson. Urbana, Ill.: National Council of Teachers of English, 1976c, pp. 57-70.

_____ . "Miscues: Windows on the Reading Process." In *Miscue Analysis: Applications to Reading Instruction,* edited by K.S. Goodman. Urbana, Ill.: ERIC Clearinghouse on Reading and Communication Skills, National Council of Teachers of English, 1977.

Goodman, K.S., and Goodman, Y.M. "Learning about Psycholinguistic Processes by Analyzing Oral Reading." *Harvard Educational Review* 47 (1977): 317-333.

Goodman, Y.M., and Burke, C.L. *Reading Miscue Inventory.* New York: Macmillan Publishing Company, 1972.

Kagan, J.; Moss, H.A.; and Sigel, I.E. "Psychological Significance of Styles of Conceptualization." In *Basic Cognitive Processes In Children, Report of the Second Conference Sponsored by the Committee on Intellective Processes Research of the Social Science Research Council,* edited by J.C. Wright and J. Kagan. Chicago, Ill.: University of Chicago Press, 1973, pp. 73-112.

Kaplan, H.A. "Relationships among Cognitive Styles, Personality Traits, and Reading Achievement at the Elementary School Level (Doctoral dissertation, Rutgers University, 1969). *Dissertation Abstracts International* 30 (1970): 4278A.

Kogan, N. "Educational Implications of Cognitive Styles." In *Psychology and Educational Practice,* edited by G.S. Lesser. Glenview, Ill.: Scott, Foresman and Company, 1971, pp. 242-292.

Ohnmacht, F.W. "Psychological Research: A Psychometric Point of View." *Journal of Reading Behavior* 3 (1970): 213-220.

Readence, J.E. *A Psycholinguistic Analysis of the Oral Reading Miscues of Impulsive and Reflective Third Grade Children.* Unpublished dissertation, Arizona State University, 1975.

Ruddell, R.B. "Psycholinguistic Implications for a Systems of Communication Model." In *Theoretical Models and Processes of Reading,* edited by H. Singer and R.B. Ruddell. Newark, Del.: International Reading Association, 1976b.

Santostefano, S.; Rutledge, L.; and Randall, D. "Cognitive Styles and Reading Disability." *Psychology in the Schools* 2 (1965): 57-62.

Smith, F. *Psycholinguistics and Reading.* New York: Holt, Rinehart and Winston, 1973.

_____ . *Understanding Reading.* New York: Holt, Rinehart and Winston, 1978.

Stone, M.K. *Correlates of Teacher and Student Cognitive Style.* Beginning teacher evaluation study, Phase II, 1973-74. ERIC ED 131 120, 1976.

Stuart, I.R. "Perceptual Style and Reading Ability: Implications for an Instructional Approach." *Perceptual and Motor Skills* 24 (1967): 135-138.

Watson, B.L. "Field Dependence and Early Reading Achievement" (Doctoral dissertation, University of California, 1969). *Dissertation Abstracts International* 31 (1970): 656A.

Wineman, J.H. "Cognitive Style and Reading Ability." *California Journal of Educational Research* 22 (1971): 74-79.

Witkin, H.A. "Individual Differences in Ease of Perception of Embedded Figures." *Journal of Personality* 19 (1950): 1-15.

Witkin, H.A.; Dyk, R.B.; Faterson, H.F.; Goodenough, D.R.; and Karp, S.A. "Field-dependent and Field-independent Cognitive Styles and Their Educational Implications." *Review of Educational Research* 47 (1977): 1-64.

Mexican American Culture in Bilingual Education Classrooms Grades 1 through 3: A Description of Three Spanish/English Programs in Texas

Paul Franklin Gonzales

Semifinalist, Outstanding Dissertations
National Advisory Council on Bilingual Education

Degree conferred May 1978
University of Texas at Austin
Austin, Texas

Dissertation Committee:
George M. Blanco, *Chair*
Rudolph F. Martin
Theodore Andersson
Melvin P. Sikes
Anna Uhl Chamot

About the Author

Dr. Paul F. Gonzales is Training Resource Specialist at the Bilingual Education Service Center in Austin, Texas. He has served as a consultant in the areas of bilingual education, classroom management, culture in the classroom, language assessment, English as a second language, and affective education. Dr. Gonzales is the author of *Training Resources Index for Bilingual Educators in Texas* (Austin: Bilingual Resource Center, 1979), fourteen Adult Performance Level modules developed for the University of Texas at Austin (1977), and texts on conversational Spanish.

SUMMARY

The purpose of this study was to determine which surface elements and deep elements of Mexican American culture were included in three Spanish/English bilingual education programs in Texas.

The findings indicate that the surface culture elements being reinforced by the majority of the programs are traditional songs in Spanish, Mexican crafts, and culinary activities. Surface culture elements receiving little reinforcement are Mexican dances and Chicano music; Mexican American history and Mexican American personalities; and folk tales, proverbs, poetry, and word play in the Spanish language. Deep culture elements were found to be reinforced on an impromptu basis rather than in organized lessons. Deep culture elements being reinforced with organized lessons were family ties, folk myths, grooming and presence, subsistence, time concept, and values. The elements having less organized discussion were esthetics, ethics, precedence, and rewards and privileges. Those elements having little or no reinforcement were ceremony, courtship and marriage, health and medicine, gesture and kinesics, ownership, rights and duties, religion, sex roles, space and proxemics, and tabu.

In summarizing the results of this study, it remains evident that transmitting or reinforcing culture in the bilingual education classroom remains one of the most misinterpreted and inadequately achieved goals of bilingual education instruction.

STATEMENT OF THE PROBLEM

Prior to the civil rights movement, the idea of biculturalism or multiculturalism was not associated with the educational process. If individuals chose to maintain more than one cultural identity, they did it of their own will and often at the expense of being socially and educationally ostracized by the majority group. The Bilingual Education Act of 1968, Title VII, Elementary and Secondary Education Act (ESEA), the first legislation of its type in U.S. educational history, attempted to redress the miseducation of ethnic minority children whose home language was other than English and whose culture was other than Anglo Saxon (Herrmann, 1975). This legislation provides for the development of greater competence in English, more proficiency in the home language, reinforcement of the home culture by the school, and increased emphasis on equal educational opportunities. The document describes bilingual education as:

> ...the use of two languages, one of which is English, as mediums of instruction for the same school population in a well-organized program which encompasses part or all of the curriculum and includes the study of the history and culture associated with the mother tongue. (U.S. Department of Health, Education, and Welfare, 1968: 1-2)

The phrase "...history and culture associated with the mother tongue" legitimatized the teaching of cultural diversity in public elementary and secondary schools. The 1974 amendment to ESEA expanded this instruction into higher education, teacher training, and vocational training.

A decade has passed since the initial legislation was approved, and the idea of cultural pluralism is having an enormous impact in areas where the needs of disenfranchised groups are beginning to be met. The world is in a state of change, and one change in particular is that of its view of the role of culture in a diverse society.

A number of thoughtful proponents of cultural pluralism in U.S. education state unequivocally that it is not enough for the school to recognize language differences; it is also necessary to accept cultural differences in order to enhance a student's achievement (Ulibarrí, 1970; Litsinger, 1973). Other educators have stated the case for cultural diversity eloquently (Ramírez, 1973; Leyba, 1973; and Hernández, 1974). Sullivan (1974) coined the term "educational culturalism" to reflect the concern for including culture in the curriculum. Castañeda, Leslie, and Ramírez (1974) demanded "cultural democracy," the basic right of the child to develop and maintain an identity based on the socialization experiences of childhood. González (1974) has developed a rationale for "culture-based and cultural context teaching" for Spanish/English bilingual programs with emphasis on the Chicano of the Southwest. Herrmann (1975) has analyzed the cultural components of six French/English bilingual programs in New England and Louisiana by using Hall's (1959) map of culture. Seelye (1974) has set forth some strategies for the foreign language teacher in his book, *Teaching Culture.* But, as of this date, little has been done to identify which elements of the Mexican American culture should be or are actually being reinforced or taught in the bilingual bicultural classroom in Texas. It would seem, therefore, that bilingual programs would profit greatly from such information.

ORGANIZATION OF THE STUDY

The organization of the study is as follows:

Chapter I. Introduction to the Study: This chapter includes a background for the study, definition of culture, a discussion of its place in bilingual education programs, and the procedures of the study.

Chapter II. Review of Related Literature: The literature reviewed is derived from the fields of anthropology, sociology, psychology, social sciences, educational curriculum, foreign language instruction, and bilingual education.

Chapter III. Description of Three Spanish/English Bilingual Programs: This chapter contains a description of the three sites involved in the study and is based on actual observation, tape recordings of the questionnaire sessions, discussions with the teachers, and examination of curriculum materials.

Chapter IV. Results of the Questionnaire: This chapter contains the findings from the questionnaire. The results from each district are presented in appropriate tables.

Chapter V. Summary and Recommendations: This chapter includes a summary of the study, summary of the findings, recommendations for program implementation, and recommendations for further research.

PURPOSE OF THE STUDY

The primary purpose of this study was to identify the elements of culture from the perspective of several disciplines and to determine the elements of Mexican American culture that are actually included in three bilingual education programs in Texas.

This study sought to accomplish the following objectives:

- To review and analyze the literature pertaining to teaching culture in the areas of anthropology, sociology, psychology, and language teaching, and to draw from it inferences for bilingual education curriculum

- To identify research and information pertaining to the teaching of culture in the bilingual classroom

- To identify the elements of Mexican American culture (surface culture and deep culture) that are reinforced or included in three Spanish/English bilingual education programs (grades 1 through 3) in Texas

- To describe cultural instruction in three bilingual education programs in Texas (grades 1 through 3)

- To make recommendations for the improvement of instructional methodologies and materials used to present elements of culture in Spanish/English bilingual education programs in Texas.

DEFINITION OF CULTURE

From a rudimentary educational perspective, Seelye's definition, "culture is seen to include everything people learn to do," (1974, p. 10) can best serve as a basic concept for this study.

Brooks (1966) divided culture into two categories—*formal culture* and *deep culture.* A more recent term, *surface culture,* has become associated with formal culture. For the purpose of this study, *surface culture* and *formal culture* are used interchangeably. Brooks refers to *formal culture* as consisting of

...the products of artistic endeavor, achievements of intellectual and artistic genius, deeds of heroic valor and concepts of lofty spirit, and various modes of significant thought, genteel living, and racial vigor. (1966, p. 4)

Deep culture, on the other hand refers to

> ... the thoughts and beliefs and actions, the concerns and hopes and worries, the personal values, the minor vanities and the half serious superstitions, the subtle gradations of interpersonal relationships as expressed in actions and words, the day-by-day details of life as it is lived.... (1966, p. 4)

At the risk of oversimplifying the terms, this study considered the tangible elements of the Mexican American culture as surface culture and the intangible elements as deep culture. Surface culture elements are those which are to an extent concrete and can be presented in a classroom situation. This category includes such items as language components, songs, dances, arts and crafts, foods, holidays, history, etc. Deep culture elements have to do with attitudes and feelings toward certain topics.

PROCEDURE

This study involved three Texas school districts offering Spanish/English bilingual education programs. The school districts selected are located in different geographic regions: the High Plains of West Texas, Central Texas, and extreme South Texas. Each site has a different percentage of Mexican American population, has different economic situations, and differs from the others in proximity to the Mexican border.

Onsite visits were made to three schools in each district. Data were gathered in a total of nine schools. The schools participating in the study were selected in consultation with the bilingual education directors of each district.

A questionnaire was administered to all available instructional personnel of the bilingual classes in grades 1 through 3. The questionnaire was administered in each school under the supervision of the researcher. Each group was also recorded on tape. These tape recordings were used in describing the attitudes and feelings of instructional staff toward Mexican American culture as well as toward the questionnaire itself. The researcher was available during the questionnaire sessions to clarify or give additional examples of the items included in the questionnaire. The results of the questionnaire were organized into thirty-three tables throughout the dissertation.

SUMMARY OF THE FINDINGS

Averages can be derived relating to the presentation or reinforcement of the cultural elements with which this study dealt. The following is an interpretation of these findings.

Surface Culture

Certain averages may be assumed concerning musical activities in the bilingual education classroom. Traditional songs in Spanish were used by 83 percent of the teachers while only 66 percent of the teachers used contemporary songs in the Spanish language. Fewer than half, 48 percent, of the teachers used *rondas* in their classroom activities. Traditional Mexican dances were taught by 31 percent of the teachers whereas only 11 percent used contemporary or popular dances in their activities.

Averages from the measurement of language arts activities show that only 68 percent of the teachers used Spanish language children's stories. Although 49 percent of the teachers indicated that they used Spanish language folktales, two sites listed only English language fairy tales that had been translated into Spanish. Sayings or *dichos* and proverbs or *refranes* were used by 31 percent of the teachers. Spanish poetry or *versos* averaged 61 percent usage while 67 percent of the teachers reported using drama and role play. Therefore, it can be assumed that approximately two-thirds of the bilingual education teachers who participated in the study emphasized children's stories, poetry and *versos,* and drama or role play in the Spanish language during their language arts activities. The cultural items given less emphasis were folktales, *dichos,* and *refranes.*

Averages for craft and culinary activities are as follows: Traditional Mexican crafts were incorporated into the art activities by 31 percent of the teachers. Only 18 percent of the classes had special art projects representative of Mexican American culture. None of the classes was exposed to contemporary Chicano artists or other Spanish-speaking artists from Latin America or Spain. The origin or history of foods related to Mexican American culture was discussed by 31 percent of the teachers while 44 percent of the teachers prepared some of the foods in the classroom.

Discussion activities provide the following averages: Mexican patriotic holidays were discussed by 51 percent of the teachers. Religious holidays related to Mexican American culture were discussed by 51 percent of the teachers, also. Personal holidays and observances were discussed by 37 percent of the teachers. Discussion of historical contributions related to Mexican Americans appears to be the least pursued activity in the bilingual education classroom. Only 5 percent of the teachers discussed the contributions of the Spanish-speaking peoples during the discovery period of Mexico, and only 2 percent of the teachers discussed the contributions of the Spanish-speaking peoples during the colonization of the southwestern United States. No discussion activities related the contributions of the Spanish-speaking peoples during the vast immigration period from Mexico, from 1910 to 1950, nor during the Chicano movement. Historical Mexican personalities were discussed by 35 percent of the teachers, while 21 percent of them discussed local Mexican American citizens.

Table 1 shows the overall averages of the sites studied. The column marked *Table* indicates the table in the dissertation proper from which the percentages were derived. Topic 1 includes both categories of Spanish language songs: traditional and contemporary. An example of the percentages shown would be: of the teachers who do teach songs in Spanish, 71 percent do so between ten and fifty minutes per week, 1 percent do so between one and two hours per week, 2 percent do so between three and four hours per week, none does so five or more hours per week, and 26 percent do so by the instructional unit. Table 1 reflects the percentages of only those teachers who are engaged in those activities listed in the table. The reader is referred to the preceding narrative to review the percentages of teachers who are engaged in these activities.

Table 1
Time Devoted to Cultural Activities
Averages of Sites Studied

		Percentages Shown				
Topic	*Table*	10-50 MPW*	1-2 HPW**	3-4 HPW**	5+ HPW**	by IU***
Songs	13	71	1	2	—	26
Rondas	14	88	1	—	—	11
Dances	15	42	—	—	—	58
Stories	17	61	16	4	10	9
Folktales	18	73	1	—	—	26
Dichos and *Refranes*	19	97	—	—	—	3
Adivinanzas	20	62	1	—	—	37
Drama and Role Play	21	58	2	—	—	40
Mexican Arts and Crafts	23	46	3	—	—	51
Discussing Mexican American Foods	24	43	5	—	—	52
Preparing Mexican American Foods	25	25	2	—	—	73
Discussing Holidays and Observances	27	33	2	—	—	65
Discussing Mexican American History	28	41	3	—	—	56
Discussing Mexican American Personalities	29	63	1	—	—	36

*Minutes Per Week
**Hours Per Week
***Instructional Unit

Deep Culture

In the category of deep or intangible cultural elements, this study dealt with twenty parameters of Mexican American culture. The responses to these items by sites are found in Table 2. Each item contains four columns. An example of the percentages shown for item 1 would be: 53 percent of the teachers do not reinforce the parameter of ceremony, of the 47 percent who do reinforce ceremony, 5 percent do so with organized lesson plans and materials while 95 percent do so on an impromptu basis as circumstances arise. Therefore, it is logical to assume that a relatively high percentage in the *Yes* column and in the *Impromptu* column would mean that that the cultural item would receive such minor attention that in reality it would not form a significant part of the teaching activities.

Consequently, the parameters of culture less frequently reinforced (those receiving between 32 and 83 percent negative responses) are

Table 2
Parameter of Culture
Averages of the Sites Studied

Do you discuss the following items in your classes?	Percentages Shown		Is your discussion organized with lesson plans or impromptu as circumstances arise?	
	No	Yes	Organized	Impromptu
1. Ceremony	53	47	5	95
2. Courtship and Marriage	83	17	1	99
3. Esthetics	21	79	21	79
4. Ethics	11	89	22	78
5. Family Ties	17	83	39	61
6. Health and Medicine	46	54	11	89
7. Folk Myths	26	74	46	54
8. Gesture and Kinesics	32	68	36	64
9. Grooming and Presence	19	81	34	64
10. Ownership	38	62	17	83
11. Precedence	23	77	28	72
12. Rewards and Privileges	18	82	14	86
13. Rights and Duties	37	63	28	72
14. Religion	54	46	19	81
15. Sex Roles	45	55	19	81
16. Space and Proxemics	67	33	3	97
17. Subsistence	18	82	40	60
18. Tabu	44	56	17	83
19. Time Concept	18	82	53	47
20. Values	15	85	31	69

ceremony, courtship and marriage, health and medicine, gesture and kinesics, ownership, rights and duties, religion, sex roles, space and proxemics, and tabu. Therefore, it can be assumed that approximately two-thirds of the bilingual education classes studied receive no reinforcement or minimal reinforcement in ten of the parameters.

The parameters of culture receiving more reinforcement than the preceding group but less than 30 percent organized discussion are esthetics, ethics, precedence, and rewards and privileges. The parameters of culture receiving the greatest amount of organized reinforcement (between 31 and 53 percent) are family ties, folk myths, grooming and presence, subsistence, time concept, and values.

IMPLICATIONS

The following points focus on changes that are pertinent to making bilingual education programs bicultural. No particular order or priority is intended by the sequence in which they are listed, since they are equally important to an effective bilingual bicultural program.

Training Bicultural Teachers

The challenge of preparing teachers who are bicultural rests upon the same institutions of higher learning that for so many years produced teachers who exemplified middle class assimilation educational theory. Higher education must meet this challenge through the following strategies:

- Incorporate reading of culturally oriented books and materials into reading requirements

- Require competencies in cultural areas

- Require a high degree of competence in the target language through practical language courses, pedagogy courses taught in the target language, field experiences in the community, or study abroad

- Design programs that correct the inadequacies shown by this study in the areas of Mexican American history, contributions of the Spanish-speaking peoples to the real world, language arts activities, and the intangible elements of the Mexican American culture.

Retraining Present Staff

Unfortunately, many unqualified yet certified teachers remain in bilingual education classrooms today. It is to be hoped that they will soon be replaced by recent graduates of institutions with adequate bilingual education preparation and training. School districts throughout the state must determine the cultural inadequacies of its teaching staff within its bilingual program and take steps to alleviate them. This process can be accomplished through self-evaluation, needs assessments, inservice education, university training, travel, involvement with social and political organizations, etc. Suggestions for improving staff inadequacies include the following:

- Provide inservice training programs with bicultural emphasis
- Revise teaching manuals and guides to include cultural topics in all subject areas
- Encourage teacher participation in culturally relevant activities in the school and community
- Involve the culture of the home in the school's teaching activities
- Compile reading lists of pertinent books, articles, and pamphlets
- Use the target language as much as possible in everyday school communication by faculty, staff, and administrators, since language is an integral part of culture.

CURRICULUM CHANGES

Curriculum development personnel need to determine the significant factors of the bilingual child's culture and incorporate those elements into the curriculum of the district. A bicultural or multicultural curriculum for any school district can be achieved by means of the following:

- Involve the cultural groups in the establishment of cultural goals and priorities
- Adapt present curriculum to reflect cultural differences and similarities
- Sequence cultural materials throughout the various grade levels.

CONCLUSION

This study sought reassurance that bilingual bicultural education programs in Texas presented both the Anglo and the Mexican American cultures as equally valued, and that the students in bilingual education classes were being instructed in two languages with reinforcement of both cultures. It is obvious that such is not the case in the majority of the classrooms involved in this study. Bilingual bicultural education in Texas occupies a compensatory status in which the sharing of culture remains a sound, but one-directional, theoretical construct.

REFERENCES

Brooks, Nelson. "Culture and Language Instruction." *Teachers Notebook in Modern Foreign Languages.* New York: Harcourt, Brace and World School Department, 1966.

Castañeda, Alfredo P.; Harold, Leslie; and Ramírez, Manuel, III. "A New Philosophy of Education." *New Approaches to Bilingual, Bicultural Education.* Austin, Tex.: Dissemination and Assessment Center for Bilingual Education, Education Service Center, Region XIII, 1974.

González, Josué M. *A Developmental and Sociological Rationale for Culture-based Curricula and Cultural Context Teaching in Early Instruction of Mexican American Children.* Doctoral dissertation, University of Massachusetts at Amherst, 1974.

Hall, Edward T., Jr. *The Silent Language.* New York: Doubleday, 1959.

Hernández, Norma G. "Multicultural Education and CBTE: A Vehicle for Reform." ERIC ED 091 386, 1974.

Herrmann, Marjorie Elmira. *Culture in French Bilingual Curricula: An Analysis of Six Title VII Program Designs from New England and Louisiana.* Doctoral dissertation, University of Texas at Austin, 1975.

Leyba, Charles F. "Cultural Identity: Problem and Dilemmas." *Journal of Teacher Education* 24 (1973): 272-276.

Litsinger, Delores Escobar. *The Challenge of Teaching Mexican-American Students.* New York: American Book Company, 1973.

Ramírez, Manuel, III. "Culturally Democratic Learning Environments: A Cognitive Styles Approach." Unpublished manuscript from Multi-lingual Assessment Project, Riverside Component, Riverside, Calif., 1973.

Seelye, H. Ned. "Teaching Cultural Concepts in Spanish Classes." ERIC ED 108 454, 1972.

_____ . *Teaching Culture: Strategies for Foreign Language Educators.* Skokie, Ill.: National Textbook Company, 1974.

Sullivan, Allen R. "Culture Competence and Confidence: A Quest for Effective Teaching in a Multicultural Society." ERIC ED 091 388, 1974.

Ulibarrí, Horacio. "Bilingual Education: A Handbook for Educators." ERIC ED 038 978, 1970.

U.S., Department of Health, Education, and Welfare. *Bilingual Education Act, Title VII, Elementary and Secondary Education Act.* Washington, D.C.: Office of Education, 1968.

_____ . *Amendment to Bilingual Education Act, Title VII, Elementary and Secondary Education Act.* Washington, D.C.: Office of Education, 1974.

The Relationship of Language Orientation and Racial/Ethnic Attitude among Chinese American Primary Grade Children

Irene Sui-Ling Kwok

Semifinalist, Outstanding Dissertations
National Advisory Council on Bilingual Education

Degree conferred May 1979
University of the Pacific
Stockton, California

Dissertation Committee:
Augustine García, *Chair*
Juanita Curtis
John Phillips
Fé María Hufana
Ezekiel Ramírez

About the Author

Dr. Irene Sui-Ling Kwok is a bilingual educator in the San Francisco Unified School District (SFUSD), where she was a curriculum specialist in the Chinese Bilingual Pilot Program for eight years. She has conducted many in-service crosscultural workshops for SFUSD teachers and paraprofessionals, and she has developed a wide variety of Chinese cultural resource materials and texts for use in bilingual classrooms.

SUMMARY

This study was designed to determine whether there was a relationship between the language orientation of Chinese American primary-grade children in the San Francisco Unified School District and their racial/ethnic attitudes. Three linguistic groups of Chinese American children were compared: (1) monolingual Chinese speakers (MCS), (2) monolingual English speakers (MES), and (3) bilingual English and Chinese speakers (BECS), as determined by a state-adopted assessment instrument.

The study determined no significant intergroup differences in *racial/ethnic classification of self and others*, nor in the *ability to see racial/ethnic similarity of Chinese models to self and fathers*. However, the BECS group was found to be significantly more accurate in *perceptions of racial/ethnic similarity to mothers*. Although the three groups were not found to be significantly different in *acceptance of Chinese* or in *bias*, they were significantly different in *acceptance of Caucasians, preference, self preference,* and *overall affective racial/ethnic attitude*. In most cases where significant differences were found, the MCS group favored a Chinese orientation, the MES group favored a Caucasian orientation, and the BECS group was relatively balanced in its attitudes.

STATEMENT OF THE PROBLEM

The issue of how the school should cope with linguistic and cultural differences is very controversial today. Traditionally, schools in the United States have attempted to eliminate these differences in order to assimilate culturally different students. As a result, many cultural groups have been affected in a variety of ways. In the case of Chinese Americans, they have tended either to adhere exclusively to Chinese culture and language, to totally assimilate as English speakers, or to develop and maintain dual language and cultural abilities. The different language orientations which are characteristic of Chinese Americans may be related to their attitudes toward themselves and other people. The present study investigated this relationship.

A historical overview of the Chinese American experience in this country discloses over 100 years of racial and ethnic discrimination. It is marked by distinct periods, during which Chinese and Chinese Americans have attempted to survive under adverse conditions. Racism against the Chinese in America, which has existed since the 1850s, developed into panic proportions in the second half of the nineteenth century and early 1900s. Institutionalized racist practices and personal prejudices have continued to exist. Chinese Americans represent a wide spectrum of linguistic and cultural orientations because of the treatment they have received in this country. Chinatowns still exist, where Chinese and Chinese Americans live their daily lives totally within a Chinese environment. Other Chinese

Americans have lost all vestiges of Chinese identity; these have become completely assimilated and speak only English. Those who developed bilingual ability have found that they are able to function either in Chinatowns or in English speaking environments. However, they may also be affected by a growing identity crisis among Chinese Americans.

Bilingual crosscultural education is partially an attempt to accommodate the linguistic and cultural differences of all students. The United States Supreme Court case *Lau* v. *Nichols*, involving Chinese American students in San Francisco, was a landmark for bilingual education as well as a major breakthrough for Chinese Americans. The development of bilingual crosscultural programs could result in the reduction of negative racial/ethnic attitudes which affect this group. Racial attitudes should be investigated to determine means for improving upon them.

PURPOSE OF THE STUDY

The present study was designed to determine the relationship between language orientation and racial/ethnic attitude among young Chinese American students. The study sought to do so by comparing the specific and overall racial/ethnic attitudes of three different Chinese American linguistic groups: monolingual Chinese speakers (MCS), monolingual English speakers (MES), and bilingual English and Chinese speakers (BECS). The specific and overall racial/ethnic attitudes provided the dependent variables for the investigation. Seven specific attitudinal forms were identified in the literature, from which the hypotheses could be formulated. The study was also designed to investigate the interactive effects of grade level and sex. The significance of this study could lie in its potential for promoting a bilingual crosscultural approach in the schools in order to reduce prejudice and develop intercultural and interracial harmony.

REVIEW OF THE LITERATURE: THEORETICAL FRAMEWORK

The literature was reviewed in four areas: (1) the relationship of language, thought, and perception; (2) attitude formation and behavior; (3) race and racial attitudes; and (4) racial/ethnic attitudes among children. Each area was reviewed with a particular focus upon the needs of this study. The investigator sought to develop continuity of thought as the review in these four distinct areas was developed. The basic results of the review are summarized as follows:

1. The interrelationship of language, thought, and perception seems to have implications for attitude development, including the development of racial/ethnic attitudes. The Sapir-Whorf Hypothesis, which proposes

that language is a guide to social reality, provides a conceptual framework in this area. Culture provides the content for language expression; both language and culture shape thoughts and perceptions.

2. Attitudes about race have historically been derived from racial concepts. These concepts vary from those which are completely physiological in nature to those which attribute nonphysical characteristics to the races. Racial attitudes include racial theories, prejudice, and discrimination. The nature of these racial forms was reviewed.

3. Studies indicate that children have developed racial/ethnic awareness and attitudes by the age of three. These attitudes become increasingly negative as children get older. They appear to be influenced by parents and other people and situations in their environment.

HYPOTHESES

Based upon a review of the literature, a research design was developed and thirteen null hypotheses were written for the study. Each of ten hypotheses involved a different kind of racial/ethnic attitude. An eleventh hypothesis measured overall affective racial/ethnic attitude. Two additional hypotheses focused on the interaction of grade level and sex with linguistic grouping to affect overall affective racial/ethnic attitude.

Hypothesis 1: There is no significant difference among the MCS, MES, and BECS groups in racial/ethnic classification ability.

Hypothesis 2: There is no significant difference among the MCS, MES, and BECS groups in racial/ethnic self-classification ability.

Hypothesis 3: There is no significant difference among the MCS, MES, and BECS groups in perception of racial/ethnic similarity to self.

Hypothesis 4: There is no significant difference among the MCS, MES, and BECS groups in perception of racial/ethnic similarity to their own fathers.

Hypothesis 5: There is no significant difference among the MCS, MES, and BECS groups in perception of racial/ethnic similarity to their own mothers.

Hypothesis 6: There is no significant difference among the MCS, MES, and BECS groups in racial/ethnic acceptance of Chinese.

Hypothesis 7: There is no significant difference among the MCS, MES, and BECS groups in racial/ethnic acceptance of Caucasians.

Hypothesis 8: There is no significant difference among the MCS, MES, and BECS groups in racial/ethnic preference.

Hypothesis 9: There is no significant difference among the MCS, MES, and BECS groups in racial/ethnic self-preference.

Hypothesis 10: There is no significant difference among the MCS, MES, and BECS groups in racial/ethnic bias.

Hypothesis 11: There is no significant difference among the MCS, MES, and BECS groups in overall affective racial/ethnic attitude.

Hypothesis 12: There is no significant difference among the MCS, MES, and BECS groups in grade level interaction with overall affective racial/ethnic attitude.

Hypothesis 13: There is no significant difference among the MCS, MES, and BECS groups in sex interaction with overall affective racial/ethnic attitude.

METHODS AND PROCEDURES

Two instruments were used for the study: the San Diego Observation Assessment Instrument (SDOAI), and the Morland Picture Interview (MPI). Existing SDOAI results in the San Francisco Unified School District were used to identify the linguistic groups. The MPI, an individual interview instrument which includes ten kinds of racial/ethnic attitudes, was the sole instrument used to gather data.

The sample consisted of 150 primary-grade (K-2) Chinese American children from five schools in the San Francisco Unified School District. These were randomly selected from among 300 children who were previously stratified into the three linguistic groups. The data were gathered at each school site, with each child being individually interviewed in a room near his or her classroom. Only one person, the investigator, conducted the interviews. English or Chinese was used to interview the children. The interviews were scored with a numerical scale designed for this study.

The data were then analyzed, using one-way Analysis of Variance (ANOVA) to test for significant difference at the 0.10 level. In cases where such a difference was found, the Scheffé test of multiple comparison was used to identify the specific differences. Two-way ANOVA were used to test the interactive hypotheses.

DEFINITION OF TERMS

Among the technical or restricted terms used in this study are the following:

- *Host (dominant) culture:* That culture which predominates in a country.
- *Traditional:* Basic orientation to the native, mother culture (that of China, Hong Kong, or Taiwan).

- *Atraditional:* The total absence of traditional cultures; assimilation by the host, or dominant, culture.

- *Dualistic:* Basic orientation to the native (Chinese) and host, or dominant, culture.

- *Monolingual:* A person who speaks only one language (i.e., a monolingual Chinese speaker or a monolingual English speaker).

- *Bilingual:* A person who speaks two languages, although perhaps not equally. In this study, the term refers to those students who are sufficiently proficient in English and Chinese.

- *Bilingual education:* The use of both the English language and another language (usually the native tongue) as mediums of instruction in the schools. It is not foreign language teaching.

- *Acculturation:* The process of socialization which introduces a second culture, usually a host culture, to members of a more traditional culture.

- *Assimilation:* The total disappearance of the native culture and its replacement by the host culture in the acculturation of a person.

- *Segregation:* Isolation of people or groups from distinct people or groups.

- *De juris segregation:* Segregation which is authorized by legal statute.

- *De facto segregation:* Segregation which exists without legal sanction.

- *Desegregation:* The removal of segregation; a physical merger of distinct people and groups.

- *Integration:* Articulation among members of distinct groups.

- *Chinese American:* A U.S. resident who is descended from Chinese immigrants.

- *Racial/ethnic:* A modifier used in this study to refer to groups, attitudes, or behaviors which are identified through either racial or ethnic criteria.

- *Racial/ethnic classification ability:* The ability of children to distinguish among members of different racial/ethnic groups.

- *Racial/ethnic self-classification:* Apparent identification of a child with a particular racial/ethnic group.

- *Perception of racial/ethnic similarity to self and to parents:* Ability of children to perceive racial/ethnic similarities of models to themselves and parents.

- *Racial/ethnic acceptance:* The willingness of children to play with children of their own racial/ethnic group or another group when no choice is involved.

- *Racial/ethnic preference:* The willingness of children to play with children of their own racial/ethnic group or another group when they are free to choose.

- *Racial/ethnic bias:* Children's evaluation of qualities among members of different racial/ethnic groups.

- *Language orientation:* The apparent language ability categorization of a given group (e.g., monolingual English speakers).

FINDINGS OF THE STUDY

The following findings were determined from the testing of the thirteen null hypotheses:

1. The cognitive racial/ethnic attitudes (abilities) of young Chinese Americans are relatively consistent, regardless of language orientation. The retention of Hypotheses 1 through 4 showed, as anticipated, that the ability of Chinese American students to accurately *classify self* (Hypothesis 1) *and others* (Hypothesis 2) according to racial/ethnic criteria and to accurately perceive *racial/ethnic similarities to self* (Hypothesis 3) *and their fathers* (Hypothesis 4) is not related to language orientation. *Perception of racial/ethnic similarity to their mothers* (Hypothesis 5), however, is related to language orientation. The BECS group was found to be significantly more accurate in its perception than either the MCS or MES group. This finding was a result of the rejection of Hypothesis 5.

2. The affective racial/ethnic attitudes of the Chinese American sample were found to be related to language orientation where anticipated and not to be related where it was not anticipated. As expected, Hypothesis 6: *racial/ethnic acceptance of Chinese* was retained, as was Hypothesis 10: *racial/ethnic bias.* Regardless of language orientation, the Chinese American children accepted and were biased toward their own people. The rejection of Hypotheses 7, 8, 9, and 11 showed that significant relationship exists between language orientation and the variables of *racial/ethnic acceptance of Caucasians, preference, self-preference,* and *overall affective racial/ethnic attitude.* In all cases, the MCS group was the most Chinese oriented and the BECS groups showed a balance of racial/ethnic attitudes. The MES group tended to shift in position, but was usually Caucasian oriented.

3. The investigation of the interactive variables of grade level and sex upon overall affective racial/ethnic attitude showed no effect of grade level interaction but a highly significant effect of sex interaction. In particular, bilingual children were found to be much more apart in overall affective racial/ethnic attitude than the children in the MCS and MES groups.

CONCLUSIONS

In the development of conclusions about the racial/ethnic attitudes of children in this study, it should be noted that these attitudes exist within a nation that has emphasized race as an important criterion. With this consideration in mind, one should not consider the findings of the present study in isolation, but rather within the context of the national situation. The subjects in this study were in kindergarten, first, and second grades. This is a very formative age, where much can be done to develop positive attitudes. The orientations shown by this study, then, are indicative of what may be found among similar groups of children outside of this particular situation. The attitudinal tendencies should serve as a starting point for diagnosis of language and attitudes among children.

As reflected in the literature, the development of racial/ethnic attitudes begins with awareness. In essence, this means the development of racial/ethnic cognitive skills. Children learn to differentiate between individuals and groups on the basis of racial/ethnic criteria. The identified cognitive forms of racial/ethnic attitudes used in this study are classification ability (self and others), and the ability to identify racial/ethnic similarities to oneself and one's parents.

Affective forms of racial/ethnic attitude reflect persons' feelings toward themselves and others. The literature has shown that these affective forms are, basically, acceptance (own groups and others), preference, self-preference, and bias. Acceptance of one's own and other groups is an indicator of self-identity. Preference for one group or another is a more complex level of attitude. One's self-identity and feelings toward both groups can result in the development of self-preference. Bias is a qualitative attitude, whereby one compares two groups according to perception of worth.

The general data on levels of racial/ethnic awareness in the present study are consistent with the literature. The ability of children to classify and self-classify according to racial/ethnic criteria is very high. However, at a very early age, children are less able to see racial/ethnic similarities in themselves and in their parents than to simply classify. This evidence suggests a hierarchy in these abilities.

Since the literature makes no reference to the affective racial/ethnic attitudes of Chinese Americans, the findings reported here have no specific basis for comparison. However, reference can be made to the studies cited in Chapter 2 of the dissertation itself regarding other non-Caucasian groups, such as Blacks and Chicanos. In general, within this study, Chinese Americans showed attitudes which identified them relatively close within their own racial/ethnic group, compared with other groups previously studied.

The reader is reminded that the present study was concerned with the comparison of linguistic groups according to the specified racial/ethnic attitudes. Although mention is made regarding the general attitudinal tendencies of Chinese American children, the focus of the study is on intergroup comparisons. These, of course, make possible the recognition of the relationships being investigated. In general, the conclusion is drawn that there is a significant relationship between language orientation and racial/ethnic attitude among Chinese American primary-grade students.

IMPLICATIONS FOR EDUCATION

The findings of this study provide serious implications for the education of Chinese American children. Early recognition and identification of racial/ethnic attitudes could help numerous children to overcome serious learning handicaps. The psychological effects of negative racial/ethnic attitudes are harmful to students in terms of their self-identity and their ability to get along with others. If the schools are to be successful in their efforts toward integration, they should strive to identify these attitudes. Once this is done, the schools can concentrate upon designing appropriate educational programs to remove the racial/ethnic barriers that divide children.

This study has determined that there is a significant relationship between language orientation and racial/ethnic attitude. After showing that Chinese American students, regardless of language orientation, can classify and distinguish very well when racial/ethnic criteria are used, the study found significant differences among the linguistic groups in the area of *racial/ethnic similarity to mothers*. Bilinguals were distinctive in this regard, as they were in *acceptance of Caucasians, preference, self-preference,* and *overall racial/ethnic attitudes*. In most cases, bilinguals were found to exhibit less pronounced racial/ethnic attitudes. The scores of the BECS group were almost always more moderate than those of the other two groups. In contrast, the MCS group showed extreme tendencies in every case where significant differences existed. The MES group wavered between Caucasian orientation and a neutral position. This may be indicative of loss of identity, with movement toward the Caucasian end of the scale. The present study suggests that bilingualism is related to a more moderate racial/ethnic attitude.

In the sex interactive hypothesis, it was shown that bilingual males and females tend to separate in their attitudes toward Chinese and Caucasians. This tendency needs to be explored further, since it was an unexpected finding of the study. Although bilinguals as a group, in this study, tend not to exhibit extreme racial/ethnic attitudes, the differences between bilingual boys and girls necessitate intensive further study.

As school programs are developed to meet the needs of Chinese American children, they should focus on the development of bilingualism. Dual language ability offers a vehicle for the development of moderate racial/ethnic attitudes. Chinese American students, then, should be provided the opportunity to become functionally bilingual in both Chinese and English. The development of healthy attitudes about their own and other racial, ethnic, and cultural groups should be an integral part of their education. Once it is determined what causes differences in attitude between bilingual boys and girls, means should be found to further improve this area.

The Performance of Bilingual Children on the Spanish Standardized Illinois Test of Psycholinguistic Abilities

Frederich McCall Pérez

Semifinalist, Outstanding Dissertations
National Advisory Council on Bilingual Education

Degree conferred April 1979
University of Arizona
Tucson, Arizona

Dissertation Committee:
Samuel A. Kir, *Co-chair*
Jeanne McCarthy, *Co-chair*
Henry Butler
Roy Blake
Gregory Aloia

"The Performance of Bilingual Children on the Spanish Version of the ITPA" by Frederich McCall Perez has appeared in *Exceptional Children*, Vol. 46, No. 7 (April 1980), copyrighted 1980 by the Council for Exceptional Children. This material is used by permission.

About the Author

A certified clinical psychologist in Arizona with a Ph.D. in learning disabilities, Dr. Fred McCall Pérez has long combined clinical and administrative activities in behavioral science with his background in bilingual special education. He is currently Director of Programs, Research, and Evaluation in the Social Behavioral Science Department at Kino Community Hospital in Tucson. Dr. Pérez has also been an associate professor working with bilingual bicultural teacher training programs for special education at San Jose (Calif.) State University, and an administrator at La Frontera Community Mental Health Center. In addition to several papers on learning disabilities and mental health services delivery to minorities, he has written *Bilingual Special Education* (Urbana, Ill.: University of Illinois Press, in press).

SUMMARY

The purpose of this investigation was to determine if bilingual children score significantly higher on a testing instrument normed in Spanish or on an English translation of the same test. Hispanic kindergarten and second grade children enrolled in school in a California community were tested on the Illinois Test of Psycholinguistic Abilities (ITPA) standardized on a monolingual Hispanic population, and its English translation.

Half the children at each grade level were tested first in Spanish and again within four days in English. The other half of the subjects were tested in English first and then Spanish. Two results indicated the following:

1. Bilingual children scored as well or better on the English translation of the Spanish ITPA. The kindergarten children scored significantly higher on the English translation on two of the ten subtests. The second grade children scored significantly higher on the English translation on four of the ten subtests and on the total score.

2. The difference between the performance of the children on the Spanish and English tests appeared to be primarily on tests in the auditory-vocal channel, rather than on tests in the visual-motor channel.

This work was the first to be used as Spanish standardized instrument, and the results raised serious questions about using Spanish instruments to test bilingual children, as the courts have mandated.

STATEMENT OF THE PROBLEM

The purpose of this investigation was to determine if bilingual Hispanic children score significantly higher on a test instrument standardized on monolingual Hispanic children or on an English translation of the same test.

During the last decade there has been increased pressure on public school systems to test bilingual children in their primary language. In California, the case of *Diana* v. *State Board of Education* (1970) required the retesting of over 22,000 Spanish-speaking children. The courts banned the use of English intelligence tests, saying they unfairly classified as handicapped some children of normal intelligence. In *Lau et al.* v. *Nichols et al.* (1973) the court mandated that the San Francisco school district provide English language instruction to approximately 1,800 students of Chinese ancestry. Here the court ruled favorably for bilingual education and committed itself to act should enforcement difficulties arise. In *Guadalupe Organization, Inc.* v. *Tempe Elementary School District* (1972) the court required retesting of bilingual children in their primary language to determine if any bilingual children had been incorrectly assigned to special education.

These cases and others have increased the demands on school districts to test bilingual children in their primary language *(Serna* v. *Portales Municipal*

Schools, 1973; Diana v. State Board of Education, 1970; United States v. Texas, 1971; Aspira of New York, Inc. v. Board of Education of the City of New York, 1972). These court decisions, however, have been based on *opinion* rather than on empirical knowledge. Actually, courts have not been presented with scientific evidence that bilingual Hispanic children score higher on tests administered in Spanish than on tests in English. Legal action, instead, reflects societal opinions. It is important to note what little empirical evidence does exist.

REVIEW OF LITERATURE

In reviewing the literature in this area, it becomes clear that there is great disparity among researchers and also among members of the court as to what *bilingual* means. "To see life," Leopold (1939) said, "bilingualism is present when two languages are used as . . . media of discourse." The court in *Aspira v. Board of Education of the City of New York,* (1972) implied that all Spanish-surnamed children are possibly bilingual and should be tested in Spanish.

Another approach to the question of bilingual children's ability was to compare their scores on group intelligence tests with standardized norms. Early researchers attempted to look at these children's test performance by administering group intelligence tests to them (Colvin and Allen, 1923; Pintner, 1923; Hill, 1936; Hirsch, 1926; Rigg, 1928; Jamieson and Sandiford, 1928; Barbe, 1933; Arsenian, 1945; Yoshioka, 1929; Mitchell, 1937; Stark, 1940). It was found that bilingual children score lower than monolingual children on group intelligence tests. The criticism of using group tests made it important to look at research utilizing individually administered intelligence tests, verbal and nonverbal.

Researchers utilizing individually administered intelligence tests often tested children in English only. That is, they did not test the same children in two languages and then compare performance (Pintner and Keller, 1922; Lester, 1923; Seidl, 1937; Spoerl, 1943; Darcey, 1946; Altus, 1953; Anastasi and de Jesús, 1953; Roca, 1955; Levinson, 1959; Kittell, 1963; and Christiansen and Livermore, 1970). These studies lead to the conclusion that bilingual children are penalized on individual verbal intelligence tests administered in English and not penalized on nonverbal individual intelligence tests administered in English.

Four studies tested bilingual children in two languages, by translating the English test into another language. Three of these four studies found that bilingual children are not penalized on individually administered intelligence tests when tested in English (Anastasi and Cordova, 1953; Hickey, 1972; Palmer and Gaffney, 1972). One study, however, (Levandowski, 1975) found that the children scored lower in English than in their, native language.

From these studies, one may conclude that it is not yet possible to answer with finality the question of whether bilingual children are penalized on individually administered verbal and nonverbal intelligence tests when tested in English.

PURPOSE OF THE STUDY

The purpose of this study was to determine whether or not bilingual Hispanic children score significantly higher on the Spanish version of the ITPA standardized on Latin American monolingual children than on an English translation of the same test. The investigation attempted to answer the following questions:

1. Is there a significant difference between kindergarten bilingual children's scores on the Spanish version of the ITPA and its English translation?

2. Is there a significant difference between second grade bilingual children's scores on the Spanish version of the ITPA and its English translation?

3. Is there a significant difference between the auditory-vocal and visual-motor channel scores of bilingual children on the Spanish version of the ITPA and its English translation?

PROCEDURE

Subject Selection

The subjects for this study were selected from the total population of children in the kindergarten and second grade bilingual program of a city in the San Francisco Bay area. There was a total of 132 children in the kindergarten and 165 children in the second grade voluntary bilingual program. The following criteria were used in selecting the bilingual subjects for this experiment:

1. All children were in the voluntary bilingual program.

2. Teacher and program assistant both agreed that the children had developed expressive and receptive use of both Spanish and English.

3. The children and parents reported that Spanish is spoken in the home.

A total of twenty-eight children met these criteria at the second grade level and twenty-six at the kindergarten level. Approximately 80 percent of the mothers and 85 percent of the fathers were born in Spanish-speaking countries. The remaining parents were born in the United States.

All subjects were from a middle class or lower socioeconomic community. Subjects' families were considered to be of low socioeconomic status if they qualified for free meals at school, to be of middle class if they did not. Approximately 28 percent of the subjects used in this study were from middle socioeconomic families and 72 percent were from lower socioeconomic families. The families of all fifty-four subjects (combined kindergarten and second grade) identified themselves to be of Spanish American culture.

Tests Used

The Spanish version of the Illinois Test of Psycholinguistic Abilities and an English translation of the Spanish version were used to test all subjects. The Spanish ITPA is not a simple translation of the English ITPA, but is an adapted test looking at the same psychological operations but standardized on monolingual Spanish-speaking children. The item analysis and tentative norms for the Spanish version were based on samples of children from Mexico, Columbia, Peru, Chile, and Puerto Rico.

Design

All subjects were tested on the Spanish ITPA and its English translation. Half of the children at each grade level were tested first in Spanish and then tested in English within four days. The other half of the subjects were tested in English first and then with the Spanish test within four days of the first test administration. All testing was done under optimum conditions in the school the child attended. Any talking before the testing was done by the examiner in the language in which the child was to be tested. The tester and researcher, who is himself Hispanic (raised in Chicago), is bilingual and biliterate. The writer also assisted in the training of testers in U.S. cities and Latin America for the purpose of developing tentative norms.

RESULTS

Kindergarten

Table 1 presents the analysis of variance (ANOVA) results for repeated measures for the total scores, raw scores on the two channels and two levels, and scores of the subtests of the Spanish version of the ITPA and its English translation using twenty-six bilingual kindergarten children. The following will be seen from this table:

1. There were no significant differences between the means of total test scores on the two versions of the test.

2. There were no significant differences between the means of the auditory-vocal channel or of the visual-motor channel on the two versions of the test.

Table 1
Raw Score Means, Standard Deviations, and Significance of Difference between Spanish Version of the ITPA and its English Translation Administered to Kindergarten Subjects (N = 26)

Subtests	Spanish		English		F Ratio	p
	Mean	SD	Mean	SD		
Total Test Means	133.39	24.15	138.59	25.17	1.45	NS
Auditory Vocal Channel Mean	52.58	17.34	55.54	17.69	.89	NS
Visual Motor Channel Mean	76.55	10.28	77.13	10.00	.09	NS
Representational Level Mean	70.58	16.96	72.71	17.93	.50	NS
Automatic Level Mean	51.45	9.66	54.52	9.48	2.22	NS
Visual Association	12.73	3.39	12.00	3.01	2.2	NS
Auditory Association	8.77	5.98	8.12	5.09	.25	NS
Visual Comprehension	14.46	4.08	13.77	3.73	.88	NS
Auditory Comprehension	7.0	3.86	9.89	3.14	10.97	<.01
Verbal Fluency	25.15	10.18	26.40	9.54	1.03	NS
Motor Expression	14.81	3.25	14.88	3.13	.03	NS
Auditory Integration	10.42	3.99	9.43	3.46	1.08	NS
Visual Integration	33.23	6.95	35.08	6.61	1.40	NS
Auditory Sequential Memory	6.15	1.95	8.27	2.63	34.36	<.01
Visual Sequential Memory	6.57	2.83	7.00	2.80	.51	NS

3. There were no significant differences between the means of the Representational Level or of the Automatic Level on the two versions of the test.

4. There were significant differences on only two of the subtests (Auditory Comprehension, p. < .01, and Auditory Sequential Memory p.<.01). *This difference was in favor of the English translation.*

In other words, these results show that for this sample of bilingual kindergarten children there were no significant differences between the two administrations of the test except on the two subtests of Auditory Comprehension and Auditory Sequential Memory. On these two tests the mean raw scores were significantly higher when the test was presented in English than in Spanish.

Second Grade

Differences between scores on the Spanish ITPA and scores on its English translation for the second grade group are presented in Table 2. This table presents the ANOVA for repeated measures for the raw scores of the total scores, scores in the two channels and two levels, and on the subtests of the Spanish version of the ITPA and its English translation using twenty-eight bilingual second grade children. The following will be seen from Table 2:

1. In contrast to the kindergarten children the second grade children showed significant differences in favor of the English translation and (a) the total test mean $(p < .05)$, (b) the representational level $(p < .01)$, and (c) the auditory vocal channel tests $(p < .01)$.

2. On the subtests there were significant differences in favor of the English translation on four of the five auditory-vocal tests (Auditory Comprehension, Auditory Association, Verbal Fluency, and Auditory Sequential Memory).

3. There were no significant differences on the five visual-motor tests.

It appears that by the time the Hispanic children of this sample reach second grade they tend to test higher on an English translation of the Spanish standardized test.

Channel Differences

Table 3 presents the stanine means of the auditory-vocal channel, visual motor channel, standard deviations, F ratio, and significance of the difference between the Spanish ITPA and the English translation administered to kindergarten and second grade subjects.

It is obvious from Table 3 that the bilingual subjects of this study, at both the kindergarten and second grade levels, scored significantly higher on tests in the visual-motor channel than on tests in the auditory-vocal channel. These results support the supposition that bilingual children are penalized on auditory-vocal tests, compared with visual-motor tests, whether the test is administered in English or in Spanish.

SUMMARY AND DISCUSSION

A Spanish version of the ITPA and its English translation were administered alternately to kindergarten and second grade Hispanic children from bilingual classes in the San Francisco Bay area. The findings were as follows:

1. The kindergarten children scored the same in English as in Spanish except for two auditory-vocal tests, on which they scored significantly higher in English.

Table 2
Raw Score Means, Standard Deviations, and Significance of Difference between Spanish Version of the ITPA and its English Translation Administered to Second Grade Subjects (N = 28)

Subtests	Spanish Mean	SD	English Mean	SD	F Ratio	p
Total Test Means	176.47	26.87	197.49	35.88	6.59	<.05
Auditory Vocal Channel Mean	74.03	22.41	94.03	26.41	8.94	<.01
Visual Motor Channel Mean	97.31	8.28	96.34	11.82	.23	NS
Representational Level Mean	99.14	19.31	112.14	25.60	9.74	<.01
Automatic Level Mean	70.20	9.36	73.95	10.56	2.25	NS
Visual Association	16.18	2.85	16.29	2.93	.04	NS
Auditory Association	12.72	8.28	17.93	7.79	4.70	<.05
Visual Comprehension	16.86	2.97	16.86	2.89	0	NS
Auditory Comprehension	12.85	5.97	15.71	6.20	4.05	<.05
Verbal Fluency	32.67	8.99	42.64	12.97	15.28	.01
Motor Expression	17.10	4.00	16.25	3.74	1.70	NS
Auditory Integration	14.14	5.49	15.61	4.51	1.25	NS
Visual Integration	44.32	4.79	44.10	6.34	.04	NS
Auditory Sequential Memory	8.18	2.31	10.68	3.13	16.40	<.01
Visual Sequential Memory	14.21	2.75	14.21	2.78	0	NS

Table 3
Stanine Means of Auditory-Vocal Channel Scores and Visual-Motor Channel Scores, together with Standard Deviations, F Ratios, and Significance of Difference between Spanish ITPA and English Translation Administered to Kindergarten and Second Grade Subjects (N = 54)

	Auditory-Vocal Channel Mean	SD	Visual-Motor Channel Mean	SD	F Ratio	p
Kindergarten (N = 26)						
Spanish	3.05	.99	4.89	1.00	70.41	<.001
English	3.40	1.13	4.90	1.15	45.74	<.001
Second Grade (N = 28)						
Spanish	3.15	1.27	5.46	1.11	77.47	<.001
English	4.11	1.59	5.43	1.31	24.22	<.001

2. The second grade children scored significantly higher on all auditory-vocal tests except one.

3. On the visual-motor tests both groups scored equally in English and Spanish, and equal to the average standardization norms.

4. Neither group scored significantly higher in Spanish on any of the ten tests of the ITPA.

5. The major deviation in scores for each group was in the auditory-vocal channel whether the test was administered in Spanish or English.

The results from this sample of Hispanic children throw doubt on the wisdom of the court decisions that require bilingual Hispanic children to be tested in the language that is predominant in the home. A more logical decision in determining placement may be to examine bilingual children with nonverbal or visual-motor tests, since these children tend to score lower in auditory-vocal or verbal tests whether the test is in Spanish or English.

Testing for educational purposes rather than placement requires a determination of specific needs. The results of this study suggest that special emphasis be placed on basic language development in either Spanish or English, or both.

REFERENCES

Altus, G.J. "WISC Patterns of a Selected Sample of Bilingual School Children." *Journal of Genetic Psychology* 83 (1953): 241-248.

Anastasi, A., and Cordova, F.A. "Some Effects of Bilingualism upon the Intelligence Test Performance of Puerto Rican Children in New York City." *Journal of Educational Psychology* 44 (1953): 1.

Anastasi, A., and de Jesús, C. "Language Development and Nonverbal IQ of Puerto Rican Preschool Children." *Journal of Abnormal and Social Psychology* 48, (1953): 357-366.

Arsenian, S. "Bilingualism in the Post-war World." *Psychological Bulletin* 42, (1945): 65-86.

Aspira of New York, Inc., v. *Board of Education of the City of New York*, 72 Civ. 4002 (S.D.N.Y., filed 20 September 1972).

Barbe, E.M. "A Study of the Comparative Intelligence of the Children in Certain Bilingual and Monolingual Schools in South Wales." *British Journal of Educational Psychology* 3 (1933): 237-259.

Christiansen, T., and Livermore, G.A. "A Comparison of Anglo American and Spanish American Children on the WISC." *Journal of Social Psychology* 81 (1970): 9-14.

Colvin, S.S., and Allen, R.D. "Mental Tests of Linguistic Ability." *Journal of Educational Psychology* 14 (1923): 1-20.

Darcy, N.T. "The Effect of Bilingualism upon the Measurement of the Intelligence of Children of Preschool Age." *Journal of Educational Psychology* 37 (1946): 21-44.

Diana v. *State Board of Education*, in *Clearing House Review* 3, No. 10 (February 1970).

Guadalupe Organization, Inc. v. *Tempe Elementary School District*, No. CIV 71-435 Phx. (D. Arizona, 24 January 1972).

Hickey, T. "Bilingualism and the Measurement of Intelligence and Verbal Learning Ability." *Exceptional Children* 39 (1972): 24-28.

Hill, H.S. "Correlation between IQs of Bilinguals at Different Ages on Different Intelligence Tests." *School and Society* 44 (1936): 89-90.

Hirsch, N.D. "A Study of Natio-racial Mental Differences." *Genetic Psychological Monographs* 1 (1926): 231-407.

Jamieson, I., and Sandiford, P. "The Mental Capacity of Southern Ontario Indians." *Journal of Educational Psychology* 19 (1928): 313-328.

Kirk, S.A.; McCarthy, J.J.; and Kirk, W.D. *Examiner's Manual. Illinois Test of Psycholinguistic Abilities.* Revised Edition. Urbana, Ill.: University of Illinois Press, 1968.

Kittell, J.E. "Intelligence Test Performance of Children from Bilingual Environments." *Elementary School Journal* 64 (1963): 76-83.

Lau et al. v. *Nichols et al.*, 414 U.S. (1973): 563.

Leopold, W.F. *Speech Development of a Bilingual Child.* Evanston, Ill.: Northwestern University Press, 1939.

Lester, O.F. "Performance Tests of Foreign Children." *Journal of Educational Psychology* 20 (1923): 303-309.

Levandowski, B. "The Difference in Intelligence Scores of Bilingual Students on an English Version of the Intelligence Test as Compared to a Spanish Version of the Test." *Illinois School Research* 11, No. 3 (Spring 1975).

Levinson, B.M. "A comparison of the Performance of Bilingual and Mono-lingual Native-born Jewish Preschool Children of Traditional Parentage on Four Intelligence Tests." *Journal of Clinical Psychology* 15 (1959): 74-76.

Mitchell, A.J. "The Effects of Bilingualism in the Measurement of Intelli-gence." *Elementary School Journal* 38 (1937): 29-37.

Palmer, M., and Gaffney, P.D. "Effects of Administration of the WISC in Spanish and English and Relationship of Social Class to Performance." *Psychology in the Schools* 9 (1972): 1.

Pintner, R. "Comparison of American and Foreign Children on Intelligence Tests." *Journal of Educational Psychology* 14 (1923): 292-295.

Pintner, R., and Keller, R. "Intelligence of Foreign Children." *Journal of Educational Psychology* 13 (1922): 214-222.

Rigg, M. "Some Further Data on Language Handicap." *Journal of Educational Psychology* 19 (1928): 252-256.

Roca, P. "Problems of Adapting Intelligence Scales from One Culture to Another." *High School Journal* 18 (1955): 124-131.

Seidl, J.C. "The Effect of Bilingualism on the Measurement of Intelligence." Unpublished doctoral dissertation. New York: Fordham University, 1937.

Serna v. *Portales Municipal Schools,* 351 F Supp. 1279 (D. N.M., 1973).

Spoerl, P.T. "The Academic and Verbal Adjustment of College-age Bi-lingual Students." *Journal of Genetic Psychology* 64 (1943): 139-157.

Stark, W.A. "The Effect of Bilingualism on General Intelligence: An Investi-gation Carried Out in Certain Dublin Primary Schools." *British Journal of Educational Psychology* 10 (1940): 78-79.

U.S. v. *Texas,* 342 F Sup. 24 (E.D. Tex. 1971); aff'd, 466 F. 2d 518 (5th Cir. 1972).

Yoshioka, J.G. "A Study of Bilingualism." *Journal of Genetic Psychology* 36 (1929): 473-479.

A Comparison of Achievement of Mexican American Children in the Areas of Reading and Mathematics when Taught within a Cooperative and Competitive Goal Structure

Juanita L. Sánchez

Semifinalist, Outstanding Dissertations
National Advisory Council on Bilingual Education

Degree conferred March 1979
University of California at Santa Barbara
Santa Barbara, California

Dissertation Committee:
George I. Brown, *Chair*
Gustavo González
Mark Phillips

About the Author

Dr. Juanita L. Sánchez is Principal of Ramona Elementary School in Oxnard, California. She has also been a counselor under ESEA Title I and coordinator of ESEA Title VII programs in the Oxnard Elementary School District. Her focus of study has been on confluent education with a bilingual bicultural emphasis, and her publications include a curriculum for teaching Spanish as a second language, implementation designs for instructional services to Lau students, and a continuum of Spanish reading skills.

SUMMARY

The purpose of this study was to determine whether there is a relationship between student achievement and specific ethnic and profile characteristics of the student and the teacher. The focus of the study were Mexican and Mexican American students enrolled in fifty-eight bilingual settings, grades kindergarten through 6.

A significant relationship was found between cooperative response and the achievement of Mexican and Mexican American students in a bilingual setting in areas of both reading and math. Mexican and Mexican American students respond negatively to a cooperative teacher in the lower grades (K-2) and positively in the upper grades (3-6). The reverse is held then to be true: Mexican and Mexican American students respond positively to the competitive teacher in the earlier grades and respond negatively to the competitive teacher in the upper grades. Influence, both positive and negative, was at the 5 percent level of significance.

A bilingual setting with a Chicano teacher who is bilingual yields positive results in the areas of reading and math. The findings further seem to indicate that the use of the language other than English within the bilingual setting is not the only factor that has a positive influence on reading and math scores. Systematic differences in social motivations and learning styles existing among different ethnic student populations would seem to contribute at a significant level.

THE PROBLEM

The Plight of the Non-English-Speaking Child

The most signal failure in U.S. education is the failure to provide equality of educational opportunity for the non-English-speaking child. The primary reason for this has been the erroneous assumption on the part of our school system that every child entering school is English speaking and therefore ready to receive instruction through and in that language; ergo, the sole medium of instruction is English. The result has been an alarming dropout rate for the non-English speaking, as well as serious academic retardation for the majority of those of limited English proficiency who do remain in school.[1]

In 1971, the U.S. Commission on Civil Rights sought to examine the degree to which schools in the Southwest were succeeding in the education of minority students, specifically the Mexican American. The commission focused on school holding power, reading ability, grade repetition, over-ageness, and participation in extracurricular activities as indicators of the extent to which the school was succeeding or failing.[2]

Findings indicated that, in California, school holding power was better than in the Southwest as a whole. Even so, fewer than two out of every three Mexican American students, or 64 percent, ever graduate. By the eighth grade, about 6 percent have already left school. (See Table 1.)

More striking than the percentage loss in California is the actual number of students involved. If the present holding power rate in the California survey area persists throughout the state, of the approximately 330,000 Mexican American students in grades 1 through 6 in 1968, about 120,000 or 36 percent will have failed to graduate from high school.[3]

The reading achievement of the Mexican American student in California is poor to begin with and does not improve in the higher grades. In California, contrary to findings in other southwestern states, reading achievement does not worsen appreciably as the children progress through school. However, more than half of all Chicano students in the California survey area are already below grade assignment by the fourth grade. (See Appendix A.)

Upon graduation, 63 percent are reading below grade level and 39 percent have not advanced beyond the tenth grade level in reading. Nearly one quarter, or 22 percent, of the twelfth grade Mexican American students in California are reading at the ninth grade level or lower. Concern is heightened by the realization that an estimated 36 percent of Mexican Americans have left school by grade 12 because of low school holding power.[4]

Severe overageness of minority students is another area of concern. The lowest proportion of Chicano students who are overage is found in California, compared with the numbers found in other southwestern states. One out of every 43 Mexican American eighth graders is two or more years overage, compared with one out of every 125 Anglos. Much of this overageness is related to the limited English proficiency of Mexican American students; in many schools in the Southwest, Mexican American children are frequently required to repeat the first grade until they are judged to have sufficient mastery of the English language to study subjects in English.

Dropout rates and overageness would appear to be closely related. In the Southwest, the degree of overageness actually decreases in the secondary schools. The percentage of Mexican Americans who are overage drops from 9.4 in the eighth grade to 5.5 in the twelfth grade. (See

Table 1
School Holding Power: California

	Grade 8	Grade 12	Enter College
Anglo	100.0%	86.7%	46.9%
Mexican American	93.8	63.8	28.2
Black	97.3	67.3	34.0

Appendix B.) It is estimated that at least 41 percent of Mexican American eighth graders who are overaged do not stay in school long enough to complete the twelfth grade.[5]

A National Problem

Scattered throughout the United States today there are approximately 5 million school children who are having difficulty in U.S. public schools because they cannot communicate in the language being used to teach them. These children are not defective or learning impaired in any sense. Their difficulty stems from the fact that they came from a background in which English is not a primary language. The Mexican American is the largest linguistic minority group in the nation (about 70 percent of the non-English-speaking population are Spanish speaking), but the problem of educating the non-English-speaking child includes many language groups other than the Spanish speaking. They range in age from six to eighteen years and represent thirty different language groups. The problem of educating the non-English-speaking child is of national concern. It is a problem affecting not merely a single language group or region, but rather the entire nation.[6]

IMPORTANCE OF THE STUDY

The mandate to improve the achievement level of Mexican American children by providing them with equitable and quality education stems from a history of legal action, federal legislation for compensatory and bilingual education, and the increasing recognition of the need to deal with the cultural attributes of the students.

Since the Bilingual Education Act (P.L. 90-247) was enacted in 1968, bilingual education has become a reality. The U.S. school is at last making room for ethnicity. In bilingual education the teacher capitalizes on the language the child brings to school. The students have already internalized the sound patterns of a language, and their written work is based on those sounds. If these sound patterns are English, the beginning instruction is in English; if they are Spanish, the instruction is in Spanish. Simultaneously with such instruction, the second language is introduced systematically. At the beginning this instruction is for a rather small percentage of the time, with large periods devoted to learning in the native language. In this phase of instruction, the sound patterns of the second language are taught before proceeding to the written language. Following this procedure, the children learn two languages well. The students' cognitive development is continued while learning a second language. Also, the children avoid the trauma of finding themselves in a world where their language and culture are suddenly denied.[7]

There is a concern that bilingual education has concentrated on establishing itself and that in most cases it has presented, in the non-English language, the same curriculum that was originally geared to the middleclass Anglo student. The concern lies in whether just using the non-English language is sufficient or whether there are other factors within the educational system of the majority culture that could be affecting the achievement level of the Chicano child.

In light of these concerns and in an effort to address the different needs Chicano children would seem to have, the investigator focused on the learning and motivational styles of these students and their effects, positive or negative, on the achievement levels in the areas of reading and math. By including information of this nature in the curriculum for the training or re-training of teachers, the educational system in a pluralistic society would advance a step in meeting the needs of these students.

DEFINITION OF TERMS

- *Bilingual setting:* A classroom designated by a school district as providing assistance for the limited- and non-English-speaking student.

- *Goal structures:* The types of interdependence existing among students. The term specifies the ways in which students relate to each other and to the teacher in working toward the accomplishment of instructional goals.

- *Cooperative goal structure:* When students perceive that they can attain their goal if, and only if, the other students with whom they are linked can obtain their goal (Deutsch, 1949). If one student achieves the goal, all students with whom the student is linked achieve the goal.

- *Competitive goal structure:* When students perceive that they can obtain their goal if, and only if, the other students with whom they are linked have failed to achieve their goal. Competitive interaction is the striving to achieve one's goal in a way that blocks all others from achieving the goal.

- *Atraditional Community:* A Mexican American community whose members are most influenced by mainstream American, middleclass values.

RESEARCH DESIGN

The present investigation was concerned with whether there is a relationship between social motivation as reflected in the goal structures within the classroom and the achievement of the Chicano student in the areas of reading and mathematics, and the nature of such a relationship. As a starting point, the investigator adopted the findings of Ramírez and Castañeda (1970, 1974) that Chicano children are field dependent compared with Anglo children who are field independent, and Kagan's (1972, 1975, 1976,

1977), Madsen's (1967, 1970, 1972), and Knight's (1977) findings indicating that differences exist between the cooperative and competitive orientation of Mexican American and Anglo children. In the study the investigator compared achievement among Chicanos in the areas of reading and mathematics when taught within a cooperative goal structure and within a competitive goal structure.

The present investigation followed a previous study by Cordero (1978) which focused on teacher training. Cordero's study (1978) took place in Oxnard, California, with teachers presently assigned to local, state, and federally funded programs designated as "bilingual settings." Forty teachers enrolled in a class entitled "Cultural Variables Affecting the Learning of Chicano Children." The teachers were divided into two groups. Both groups were exposed to the same readings; that is, findings of research in the area of cooperation and competition as it relates to the Chicano child.

One group was exposed to a confluent intervention designed to develop cooperative strategies. This intervention included the three components of self-science, Gestalt learning theory, and group process. The design was presented with an emphasis on competitive and cooperative behavior patterns and how these patterns emerge in teaching. Participants were exposed to a highly competitive situation and then allowed to do a cooperative project. They were then given the opportunity to design a series of cooperative activities for their classrooms while working in the context of a support group which provided feedback and a safe environment to experiment. As part of the self-science, participants were asked to keep a journal of their interior dialogues for each situation. Gestalt learning theory consisted of an introduction concentrating on readiness exercises rather than a therapy situation. These exercises were designed to increase effective and authentic communication. Working in dyads and small groups, teachers participated in exercises such as: "Tell me how you are terrific"; "Tell me how you suffer"; "I", "You", "It" monologues; top-dog/underdog exercises; and practice in giving the others feedback.

The three components of the teacher training program follow the Yeomans model. The first part involving self-science is the innermost circle, the intrapersonal domain. Gestalt theory, involving self-awareness as well, was directed toward communication with the other or the interpersonal domain. The extrapersonal domain, the outer circle, would deal with the functioning of the group.

For the second group, readings were provided in the areas of cooperation and competition, but delivery was the traditional lecture and discussion approach. The following topics were covered in the readings:

1. The status of the Chicano and the internal and external variables contributing to that status

2. Culture, the curriculum and the teacher; how culture is transmitted explicitly and implicitly; the school as an acculturating institution

3. Locus of control; is the Chicano fatalistic?

4. Sex roles, relationships to authority: a function of socioeconomic status, culture, sex? How are these roles and relationships reflected in the educational setting?

5. Cooperative versus competitive learning styles

6. Implications of cooperative and competitive learning styles for the classroom

7. Field dependence/independence and implication for the classroom.

The present study, following that of Cordero (1978), explored relationships between achievement of Mexican, Mexican American, and Anglo American students in reading and math and the competitive motivations and behaviors exhibited by teachers, and their use of cooperative or less cooperative goal structures within the classroom. The major concern was the achievement of the Mexican and Mexican American student; however, in order to explore student achievement in light of the research cited previously, it was essential that teachers' roles and teachers' styles, both teaching and interpersonal, be examined.

FORMULATION OF OPERATIONAL HYPOTHESES

Following the review of the literature on cooperation and competition among Mexican, Mexican American, and Anglo American children, the following hypotheses were formulated for investigation in the present study:

Hypothesis 1. There is no relationship between the (1) teachers' cooperative self-perception, (2) cooperative response in a dilemma situation, or (3) ability to provide cooperative learning opportunities in the classroom, and the achievement of Mexican students in the areas of reading and math.

Hypothesis 2. There is no relationship between the (1) teachers' cooperative self-perception, (2) cooperative response in a dilemma situation, or (3) ability to provide cooperative learning opportunities in the classroom, and the achievement of Mexican American students in the areas of reading and math.

SUMMARY OF FINDINGS

The purpose of this study was to determine whether there is a relationship between student achievement and specific ethnic and profile characteristics of the student and the teacher. Ramírez and Castañeda's (1974) research provided a theoretical base for addressing this question. One aspect of their research on field dependence/field independence, that is, cooperative versus competitive interpersonal styles, was selected for further investigation. This study investigated the relationship between ethnicity and achievement within cooperative versus less cooperative goal-structured classrooms.

The focus of the study were Mexican and Mexican American students enrolled in fifty-eight bilingual settings in grades kindergarten through 6. To determine if there was a relationship between student achievement and specific ethnic and profile characteristics of the student and the teacher, the independent variables, were identified. Since the primary concern of the study was the achievement of Mexican and Mexican American students, classification was made in the following manner:

A: non-English-speaking student.

B: limited-English-speaking student.

C: bilingual or fluent English-speaking, Spanish-surnamed student achieving below Q_2. (Q_2: fiftieth percentile on national norms for tests used.)

D: bilingual or fluent English-speaking, Spanish-surnamed student achieving above Q_2.

E: fluent English-speaking, non-Spanish-surnamed student.

The independent variables with respect to the teachers were as follows:

- *Cooperative response*—This was determined by teacher response as measured in the three-instrument design by Cordero (1978). (Found in text of present dissertation.)

- *Teacher training*—Three groups were identified: Group One had received the confluent training; Group Two received the didactic training; and Group Three served as the control group and received no training. (Overview of confluent and didactic training is found in text of present dissertation.)

- *Ethnicity*—The model made reference to the teachers' being Chicano/Chicana.

- *Grade level*—The grade level taught by teachers included in the study was identified.

Each independent variable was analyzed separately from the dependent variable, as it became evident that analysis of a general profile of independent variables and the dependent variable would not be appropriate. To analyze the data so as to include all the information at hand, a multiple regression prediction technique was used. The group of independent variables included were only those that contributed to the model and were significant at the 5 percent level. Post scores on the California Test of Basic Skills (CTBS) in English reading and math were used as the dependent variable. In identifying cooperative response Cordero (1978) used three instruments: an Observation instrument, a Prisoner's Dilemma Game (PDG), and a Behavior Descriptive Questionnaire (BDQ). Since each instrument yielded different magnitudes of cooperative response for all teachers, six models were necessary, three for post-reading regression and three for post-math regression.

INTERPRETATION OF RESULTS

The constant term was significant at the 5 percent level across the six models. Cooperative response on the Observation instrument relates in a positive way at a 5 percent level of significance to the post-reading and post-math scores. In the first three models, students in categories A, B, and C obtained negative results on post-test reading scores. This, however, was expected since the testing instrument was in English. The progression from classification A to C (English speaking) decreased in negative influence as reading or speaking ability improved. Since the sample of students was taken from a bilingual setting, this result would indicate a steady sequential acquisition of English as a second language. The category C student, though still achieving below Q_2, showed a steady progression towards the mean. The same progression was evident in the post-math regression.

It was expected that with succeeding generations the cognitive style of Mexican American children would become increasingly field independent with greater exposure to the influence of Anglo American culture (Knight and Kagan, 1977; Ramírez and Castañeda, 1974; Dershowitz, 1971). The findings of the present study did not support this view. On the contrary, the findings were similar to those of Buriel (1975), who looked at first, second, and third-generation Mexican Americans and found second and first generations to be more field independent and closer to the Anglo American norm of greater field independence. Analyzing the data it is evident that a cooperative teacher has a negative influence on post-reading and post-math scores in the lower grades and a positive influence in the upper grades. It would seem then, that the Mexican and Mexican American students experience greater success in the lower grades (K-2) with a competitive teacher, and in the higher grades with a cooperative teacher. This is a direct reversal of the acculturation model. The positive influence of category D student and a cooperative teacher further supports the reversal, for the D student would represent Ramírez and Castañeda's (1974) atraditional community, and Buriel's (1975) third generation students who have become field dependent in their style of learning and more responsive to the cooperative teaching style. Buriel sees third-generation Mexican Americans acculturating more to the life style of the *barrio* or community rather than to the Anglo American culture. The findings in this study would tend to support Buriel's theory of greater field independence with first- and second-generation students and greater field dependence with third-generation students.

CONCLUSIONS

On the basis of the findings in the present study, the operational hypotheses stated in the research design may be rejected. A significant relationship was found between cooperative response and the achievement of Mexican and Mexican American students in a bilingual setting in both the areas of reading and math. Mexican and Mexican American students respond negatively to a cooperative teacher in the lower grades (K-2) and positively in the upper grades (3-6). The reverse then is held to be true: Mexican and Mexican American students respond positively to the competitive teacher in the earlier grades and respond negatively to the competitive teacher in the upper grades. Influence, both positive and negative, was at the 5 percent level of significance.

The findings would seem to indicate that confluent or similar training can contribute to raising the teachers' level of awareness of the needs of Mexican and Mexican American students, seeing them as whole persons and recognizing their cognitive and motivational learning styles within the different grade levels in the educational process. The training of teachers should include an awareness of preferred goal structures and strategies by which goal structures may be implemented in the classroom. Rather than matching students who prefer cooperative goal structures to teachers who may be competitive in their approach, teachers should receive training in both approaches in order to enable them to utilize appropriate goal structures that respond to the needs of students at different grade levels.

There would seem to be a need for sensitivity to both cooperative and competitive modes and for applying the appropriate mode with students in various content areas. The results of the present study indicate that math might be taught confluently and reading didactically, with the exception of the category D student who responds positively to a confluent teacher. It appears that Mexican and Mexican American students prefer competitive motivational style and goal structures in the lower grades and cooperative motivational style and goal structures in the upper grades. The reliability and validity of the instruments used in identifying cooperative motivational style have not been established at present. Further research is needed in this area, using either instruments that are more fully refined or tests that are more appropriate to measure the behaviors under investigation.

The continuous progression toward the norm in both reading and math would seem to indicate that bilingual settings assist the student in the acquisition of reading skills in English. However, data indicating whether this acquisition is greater than in a monolingual setting is not available because of lack of a comparison group. Further research is needed.

A bilingual setting with a Chicano teacher who is bilingual yields positive results in the areas of reading and math. The negative influence in reading scores with the category A student is cancelled by the fact that this influence can be primarily attributed to the language of the test—i.e., testing is in English for students receiving instruction in Spanish. The findings further seem to indicate that the use of the language other than English within the bilingual setting is not the only factor that has a positive influence in reading and math scores; motivational learning styles also seem to contribute at a significant level.

RECOMMENDATIONS

These recommendations for further research are based on the findings and conclusions drawn in the preceding section.

1. A replication of the study should be made to identify teachers' preferred teaching style using instruments that have more explanatory power than the instruments used by Cordero (1978).

2. Followup research is needed to determine whether students were in effect competitive in their motivational style in the lower grades, or just responding to a competitive style.

3. Further research is needed using more clearly defined bilingual classes, e.g., Title VII programs, and comparing these classes with non-Title VII classes. This would enable the investigator to include as a variable the bilingualism of both the teacher and the students being taught in the language other than English, and to allow for specific analysis of the motivational and cognitive learning styles and their relationship to achievement.

4. Further research is needed in the area of bilingual education, comparing clearly defined bilingual classes with nonbilingual classes, and using as the independent variable the use of the language other than English in the instructional program.

5. Although students classified as A, B, or C seem to demonstrate steady progression away from the negative influence of not knowing the language of instruction that is being tested, there is no evidence that this is an effect of the bilingual setting or a process of natural maturation through contact with the dominant culture. More research is necessary in the area specifically involving bilingual education.

6. Longitudinal studies are needed using matched comparison groups to determine the kinds of students who respond to a confluent approach in teaching and the age levels at which this response is maximized.

The task is left for future research to systematically explore and further ascertain whether the types of learning environment provided in schools are more or less effective, given differences in the relative dominance of various motives.

NOTES

1. Manuel Ramírez III, "Cultural Democracy: A New Philosophy for Educating the Mexican American Child," *National Elementary Principal* 50, No. 2, 1970.

2. Albar A. Peña, "Report on the Bilingual Education Program," Title VII, ESEA, *National Conference on Bilingual Education* (April 1972), pp. 221-224.

3. Albar A. Peña, Mari Luci Jaramillo et. al., "Bilingual Education," *Today's Education* 64, No. 1 (January-February 1975).

4. Mexican American Education Series, Report II, *The Unfinished Education, Outcomes for Minorities in the Five Southwestern States* (October 1971), p. 7.

5. Ibid., p. 14.

6. Ibid., p. 38.

7. T. Yeomans, "Toward a Confluent Theory of the Teaching of English" (unpublished dissertation, University of California, Santa Barbara, 1973).

Appendix A
Estimated Reading Levels in California

| | Percent below Grade level | | | | | % at Grade Level | Percent above Grade level | | |
	Total % below	More than 3 years below	2 to 3 years below	½ to 2 years below			½ to 2 years above	More than 2 years above	Total % above
Fourth Grade									
Anglo	27.0%	1.8%	5.1%	20.1%		43.3%	22.4%	7.4%	29.8%
Mexican American	52.1	6.0	12.4	22.7		34.1	11.3	2.6	13.9
Black	55.0	6.5	14.5	34.0		29.0	12.6	3.3	15.9
Eighth Grade									
Anglo	27.1	4.7	6.9	15.5		36.2	22.0	14.7	36.7
Mexican American	57.2	17.3	17.5	22.4		25.4	12.4	5.0	17.4
Black	55.0	9.9	17.1	28.0		25.1	12.5	7.3	19.8
Twelfth Grade									
Anglo	34.1	8.1	10.3	15.7		34.9	16.9	14.1	31.0
Mexican American	62.8	22.1	16.6	24.1		20.6	11.6	5.0	16.6
Black	58.7	18.9	20.2	19.6		22.2	10.9	8.3	19.2

(From Report of the United States Commission on Civil Rights, October 1971)

Appendix B
Severe Overageness

Percent of Pupils Two or More Years Overage
by Grade, State, and Ethnicity

Ethnic Group	Grade	Arizona	California	Colorado	New Mexico	Texas	Total
Anglo	1	0.7	0.9	0.7	0.4	0.7	0.8
	4	1.2	0.7	0.5	2.7	1.3	1.0
	8	1.1	0.8	0.6	2.3	2.1	1.2
	12	1.4	0.1	2.5	1.7	4.9	1.4
Mexican American	1	2.5	1.7	2.1	1.7	6.6	3.5
	4	5.6	2.1	2.3	5.5	12.0	6.9
	8	11.8	2.3	1.5	10.8	16.5	9.4
	12	10.9	2.3	3.9	6.8	10.5	5.5
Black	1	1.5	0.7	0.9	...	3.2	1.2
	4	1.3	0.7	0.7	2.0	6.1	1.8
	8	3.0	0.3	...	1.8	6.7	2.1
	12	5.5	1.9	5.4	9.1	4.6	4.4

(From Report of the United States Commission on Civil Rights, October 1971)

REFERENCES

Buriel, Raymond. "Cognitive Styles among Three Generations of Mexican-American Children." *Journal of Cross-Cultural Psychology* 6, No. 4 (December 1975).

Cordero, Diane. "The Effects of a Confluent and Didactic Training Component on Mexican-American and Anglo-American Teacher Cooperation." Unpublished Ph.D. dissertation, University of California at Santa Barbara, July 1978.

Dershowitz, Z. "Jewish Subcultural Patterns and Psychological Differentiation." *International Journal of Psychology* 6, No. 3 (1971): 223-231.

Deutsch, M. "A Theory of Cooperation and Competition." *Human Relations* 2 (April 1949): 129-131.

Kagan, Spencer, and Romero, Clarence. "Non-Adaptive Assertiveness of Anglo-American and Mexican-American Children of Two Ages." *Journal of Personality and Social Psychology* 24 (1972): 214-228.

_____, and Carlson, H. "Development of Adaptive Assertiveness in Mexican and United States Children." *Developmental Psychology* (1975): 71-78.

_____, and Zahn, Lawrence. "Field Dependence and School Achievement Gap Between Anglo-American and Mexican American Children." *Journal of Educational Psychology* 67, No. 5 (1975): 643-650.

_____, and Romero, Clarence. "Non-Adaptive Assertiveness of Anglo-American and Mexican-American Children of Two Ages." *Inter-American Journal of Psychology* 1976 (in press).

_____, and Avellar, Joseph. "Development of Competitive Behavior in Anglo-American and Mexican-American Children." *Psychological Reports* 39 (1976): 191-198.

Knight, George P., and Kagan, Spencer. "Acculturation of Prosocial and Competitive Behaviors Among Second and Third Generation Mexican-American Children." *Journal of Cross Cultural Psychology* (September 1977).

Madsen, M.C. "Cooperative and Competitive Motivation of Children in Three Mexican Sub-Cultures." *Psychological Reports* 20 (1967): 1307-1320.

_____, and Shapiro, A. "Cooperative and Competitive Behavior of Urban Afro American, Anglo-American, Mexican-American and Mexican Village Children." *Developmental Psychology* 3 (1970): 16-20.

_____, and Kagan, Spencer. "Experimental Analysis of Cooperation and Competition of Anglo-American and Mexican Children." *Developmental Psychology* 6, No. 1 (1972): 49-69.

Peña, Albar A. "Report on the Bilingual Education Program." Title VII ESEA, National Conference on Bilingual Education, April 1972.

Ramírez, Manuel, III, and Castañeda, Alfredo. "Cultural Democracy: A New Philosophy for Educating the Mexican-American Child." *National Elementary Principal* 50, No. 2 (November 1970).

_____, *Cultural Democracy, Bicognitive Development and Education.* New York: Academic Press, 1974.

Aspira v. Board of Education of the City of New York: A History and Policy Analysis

Isaura Santiago Santiago

Semifinalist, Outstanding Dissertations
National Advisory Council on Bilingual Education

Degree conferred May 1978
Fordham University at Lincoln Center
New York, New York

Dissertation Committee:
John B. Poster, *Chair*
Jay Sexter
Sayre Uhler

"Aspira v. *Board of Education of the City of New York:* A History and Policy Analysis," by Isaura Santiago Santiago, has appeared as part of *A Community's Struggle for Equal Educational Opportunity:* Aspira *v.* Bd. of Ed., by Isaura Santiago Santiago, published by Educational Testing Service in 1978 and available through its Office of Minority Education at a cost of $3.75. This material is reproduced by permission.

About the Author

Dr. Isaura Santiago Santiago is Associate Professor of Education and Director of Programs in Bilingual Education at Teachers College of Columbia University, New York City. An experienced bilingual teacher trainer and director of various bilingual research and development efforts at Hunter College, Fordham University, and City College of New York, Dr. Santiago has also been involved in alternative educational programs and family and community education. She has held such positions as Deputy Executive Director of Aspira of New York, Executive Director of the Puerto Rican Education Task Force of New York State, and board member of the PRACA Bilingual Day Care Center and Child Welfare Project. Her research and publications investigate the areas of language policy planning and implementation in bilingual education.

OVERVIEW

In recent years, policies and practices determining the education of minority language children[1] and those of limited or no English proficiency[2] have been the subject of much debate. Forums for these debates have included schools, communities, legislatures, courts, universities, and educational literature.

The literature abounds with: (1) the documentation of the under-achievement of these children (children of Spanish-speaking background[3] in particular)[4] (2) the proposed program models for their instruction,[5] and (3) the methods and materials for improved language instruction.[6] Though the literature is neither exhaustive nor definitive with regard to even these areas of performance and instruction, there are a number of areas in which the literature is particularly sparse.

This study addressed the weakness of the research literature in two such areas: the inattention to the historical and sociopolitical framework of the issues of educating children of limited or no English-speaking ability,[7] and the absence of studies of more complex matters pertaining to institutional language-of-instruction policy and the process of policy making[8] and policy change. Specifically, this study looked at the sociopolitical and historical background of policies determining the language of instruction for children of limited English proficiency in New York City schools prior to 1972. It also analyzed the impact of the resulting landmark legal agreement on language of instruction and related policies implemented between 1974 and 1976. Policies related to the language-of-instruction policy that were affected by the agreement and included in the study were: minimum educational standards, parental rights, personnel, language assessment, and finance.

In 1974 the Board of Education of the City of New York (the Board), a school district with one of the largest concentrations of minority language children in the United States, signed a landmark agreement with Aspira of New York (Aspira), a Puerto Rican community agency. The agreement, legally termed a consent decree,[9] was an outgrowth of a suit brought by Aspira and a class of children of limited English-speaking ability: *Aspira of New York, Inc., et al.* v. *Board of the City of New York et al. (Aspira* v. *Board of Education, or Aspira).*[10] The consent decree required that by 1975 the Board implement a bilingual educational program for "all children whose English language deficiency prevents them from effectively participating in the learning process and who can more effectively participate in Spanish"[11] in every local school district in New York City. As a result of this agreement, many changes in policies affecting the education of children of limited English proficiency in New York City schools occurred, particularly during the two years following the signing of the consent decree.

This study of *Aspira* v. *Board of Education:* (1) analyzed the complexity of institutions and forces that were involved in determining language-of-instruction policies and practices in New York City public school prior to the suit; (2) placed within a historical framework the efforts of two community organizations, Aspira and the Puerto Rican Legal Defense and Education Fund (PRLDEF), to change language-of-instruction policies; (3) reconstructed the issues raised during the suit's litigation regarding the education of children of limited English proficiency; and (4) summarized the impact of the consent decree on specific policies related to the implementation of the bilingual program that was agreed to—including policies regarding minimum educational standards, language assessment and grouping, personnel, finance, and parental rights.

Aspira, the Organization

Aspira is a community agency that has as its goal the social advancement of the Puerto Rican community through the education of its youth. Its focus is on high school retention and college placement and retention—though services that are indirectly associated with these also are provided.[12] *Aspira* is the Spanish word for *aspire*. Founded in New York in 1961 by Antonia Pantoja and other Puerto Rican leaders concerned about the community's future,[13] the agency's operation originally was made possible by grants from private foundations and corporations.[14] Its services first were offered out of one small office in Manhattan and later expanded to four borough offices.[15] In 1968 Aspira of America was founded, thereby establishing affiliated offices in New Jersey, Pennsylvania, Chicago, and San Juan, with central offices in New York City.[16] Today, Aspira's major efforts depend on government funding, though substantial funds are received from private foundations and corporations.[17]

Aspira has worked toward providing counseling, tutoring, financial aid, parent workshops, cultural reinforcement activities, and a wide variety of programs and services for Puerto Rican youths and their families.[18] Through the years, thousands of Hispanic students have taken advantage of these services. In fact, Aspira has witnessed an increased need and demand for these services.[19]

The Suit

On 20 September 1972, Aspira filed suit against the Board of Education of the City of New York, claiming that 182 thousand Puerto Rican children of limited or no English proficiency enrolled in New York City schools had been denied the right to equal educational opportunity[20] by the Board.[21] The discrimination suffered by the class of children was alleged to have been a function of their ethnicity and language.[22] The Puerto Rican Legal Defense and Education Fund (PRLDEF), attorneys for the plaintiffs, argued that children of limited or no English proficiency were precluded from fully participating in the learning process because they were unable to understand their teachers or their texts.[23] The PRLDEF claimed that the Board had failed to provide any or adequate pedagogical programs or services to meet the children's special linguistic and cultural needs.[24] Aspira petitioned the court to order the Board to implement a bilingual education program,[25] the only program model that Aspira felt adequately addressed the complex educational needs of the class of 182 thousand children.

The *Aspira* v. *Board of Education* consent decree, an agreement signed by both parties on 29 August 1974, provided that the Board would: (1) implement the stipulated bilingual education program,[26] (2) identify and classify those children whose English language deficiency prevented them from fully participating in the learning process and who could participate more effectively in Spanish, (3) promulgate a policy of minimum educational standards to all districts and high schools in the school system,[27] and (4) apply its maximum efforts to obtain the necessary number of teachers and the funds required to implement the program by 4 September 1975, to all children entitled to the program as defined by the decree.[28] The consent decree constituted a policy statement; however, the specific policies in areas such as minimum educational standards, personnel, assessment, finance, and parental rights were formulated (in some cases after consultation between both parties)[29] during the two-year period following the signing of the consent decree.

SIGNIFICANCE OF THE STUDY

Inasmuch as even the most conservative figures have placed the number of minority language children in the United States at over 1.6 million, the dimensions of the educational issues relevant to policies determining the education of these children are substantial.[30] Adding impetus to the nature and scope of the debate on this policy issue have been developments in the area of law and civil rights, which have included: (1) the 1970 guidelines of the Civil Rights Act of 1964,[32] (2) the 1974 Supreme Court decision in *Lau* v. *Nichols*,[33] and (3) the 1974 court-ordered consent decree resulting from *Aspira* v. *Board of Education*. As a result of these developments, federal policy now requires that hundreds of federally aided school districts throughout the country with substantial numbers of minority language children[34] implement special educational programs that address their linguistic needs and ensure their full participation in the learning process.[35] Noncompliance with these federal regulations could result in the withdrawal of federal aid.[36]

This study of selected factors related to language-of-instruction policies in New York City schools prior to *Aspira* and the suit's history and policy impact has the potential of contributing to the field. It offers school systems involved in the process of planning or implementing programs an understanding of the complexity of legal and policy issues related to the educational rights of children of limited English-speaking ability. The study offers a sociopolitical and historical framework within which to place these issues. The study might also suggest to court officials the lack of efficacy of changing school systems through legal imposition of broad-based policies that delineate the language of instruction for children of limited English proficiency without concomitant changes in other policy areas such as finance, personnel, testing, and grouping.

For community-based interest groups, including parent groups, teacher groups, and social-planning or advocacy groups, the study offers an analysis of the roles played and strategies implemented by Aspira and other community interest groups in their efforts to use the courts to change educational policies. For potential plaintiffs, including children and their guardians in other cities and states who feel that educational institutions are not complying with their obligation to provide equal educational opportunity, Aspira's experience may offer insights, alternatives, and precautionary considerations from which to draw. ·

Finally, an analysis of the policy impact of the suit and the resulting consent decree is important inasmuch as the consent decree has served as a legal precedent and a pedagogical model for court officers, government officials, and community and educational interest groups throughout the country. Approximately 80 thousand children initially were identified as eligible for the consent-decree program.[37] This is one of the country's largest populations of children of limited English proficiency under one urban educational jurisdiction.

METHODOLOGY

This study examined policy precedents and other factors which contributed to the *Aspira* v. *Board of Education of the City of New York* suit and its impact on policies and practices in educating children of limited English proficiency. In reconstructing the historical background of the litigation, the study placed the suit within the context of changing language-of-instruction policies in the United States and Puerto Rico. It analyzed aspects of the Puerto Rican community's experience on the mainland and the position taken by community interest groups on educational issues. The investigation then identified policy precedents for educating children of limited English proficiency, particularly language-of-instruction policies on city, state, and federal levels which predated the litigation.

The study presented policy issues within the context of the suit's litigation. Differences were analyzed in policy positions taken by Aspira, the officials of the board of education, their legal counsel, and the court. The bases for accommodation, negotiation, and the resolution of disputes were discussed and documented. Finally, the study analyzed the process and product of policy determination. These reforms were generated during the first two years of the decree's implementation and were largely the result of either court intervention or further negotiation and consultation between the litigating parties.

In examining the differences in policy goals and means of implementation recommended by the Board, Aspira, and at times, the court, the study relied on an abundance of litigation documents, testimony, and reports submitted to the court by both parties. These articulated the position taken by the Board, its top administrators, and its legal counsel on the policy issues studied. Interviews were also conducted with key individuals who, at varying points, played a role in the process of policy reform and who, in many cases, were not called upon to testify. Insight into the policy change process was possible due to the author's access to the files of key individuals and groups; particularly important were the confidential files of Aspira and the PRLDEF. These contributed knowledge about personalities, strategies, and confidential negotiations between the litigants. Such access is rare, particularly in cases such as this where, at this writing, the suit is still in litigation and the court retains jurisdiction over the consent decree's implementation.

Included in the records of Aspira and the Puerto Rican Legal Defense and Educational Fund (PRLDEF) were internal documents and correspondence between the litigants. In addition, there were internal board of education documents pertinent to the education of children of limited English proficiency in New York City schools which were obtained during fact-finding, the discovery process, the interrogation of witnesses for both sides, and from documents retrieved under writ of public information. These and many other papers were often not entered into the court record and were, therefore, inaccessible to the public. These materials, together with the literature on the subject, the relevant newspaper articles of the period studied, and personal interviews, made possible the reconstruction of the history of the suit, the forces contributing to the policy change process, and an analysis of the ultimate policy determinations.

The analysis of the causes and determinants of policy change in some cases resists investigation that is based on controlled and rigidly defined analytic models having as their goal inferential projections to other situations. As was evident in the policy change process studied here, the study of policy change must provide for the consideration of: (1) the multiplicity of variables which come to bear on a given problem in the field of education, and (2) the complexity of government and public institutions and interest groups which play a role in educational policy making. This analysis holds special relevance to future research which seeks a better understanding of the role minority groups and the courts have played as agents in the process of policy change. It also provides insight into the process of policy determination and policy implementation. These are areas in which there is a critical need for meaningful educational research.

The study has laid the groundwork for the next necessary step, a study of the impact new policies have continued to have. These policy issues and related variables, many of which have been considered here, must be approached systematically in developing a research design to measure their impact on the children participating in the program.

CONCLUSIONS

The research summarized here drew the following conclusions:

1. Prior to *Aspira* v. *Board of Education* there were many complex forces and factors operating on city, state, and federal levels which served, in effect, as the case's social, legal, and institutional underpinnings.

2. Litigation brought by a Hispanic advocacy group with the goal of changing existing educational practices was an effective policy change strategy for a portion of the class of children of limited English proficiency which it initially sought to represent.

3. Carrying out the litigation, consultation, and negotiation that the suit demanded required the investment of substantial, sustained, and long-term efforts on the part of the litigating parties for more than a four-year period.

4. The suit resulted in policy reform and accommodation in areas including minimum educational standards, parental rights, assessment, personnel, and finance.

5. Had the consent decree incorporated more specific policy statements, its implementation might have been expedited.

6. Aspira and the PRLDEF's consistent monitoring of the consent decree's implementation resulted in 1976 in contempt proceedings and judicial reviews which were effective in increasing the board's compliance with the decree.

7. Had the PRLDEF not insisted on a court-ordered consent agreement which included a timetable for implementation, the specific elements of the bilingual education program to be implemented, and basic criteria for personnel in the program, the program's implementation would have suffered a serious setback between 1974 and 1976 as a result of the city's financial crisis.

8. As a result of *Aspira* v. *Board of Education*, by the end of the 1975–76 school year, a broad-based bilingual educational program was in operation in New York City public schools, serving over 58 thousand pupils and involving over fifteen hundred bilingual personnel.

RECOMMENDATIONS AND REMAINING POLICY ISSUES

A number of recommendations which may have an impact on future policy determination emerge from the study. These highlight the need for further research, since the first critical years of the implementation phase of the consent decree program have elapsed and there is a need for a longitudinal study across all educational levels to investigate the effects of the consent decree program. Factors to be considered include pupil achievement in subject areas, language development in both languages, program design, program administration, and personnel. Other important questions to be answered through systematic, long-range study include the following:

1. How effectively does the Language Assessment Battery (LAB) identify children who do not fully participate in the educational process because of lack of proficiency in English? This would include looking at the educational experience of children who scored above the twentieth percentile on the English LAB.

2. Are ethnic minority, bilingual teachers more effective than nonethnic and monolingual teachers in educating minority language children, and if so, to what extent and in what ways?

3. How do consent decree participants compare to those Hispanic children who scored below the twentieth percentile in the LAB-English but scored yet lower on the LAB-Spanish? These children were entitled to the program.

4. How do pupils who opted out of the consent decree program (either by choice or parental withdrawal) compare with students who participated in the program?

5. How does the progress of students participating in magnet school programs (those programs within a district that bring together children who had been attending school in which there was not sufficient number of entitled children to implement a complete program) compare with the achievement of those children who attend neighborhood school programs?

6. Why do parents withdraw their children from the program? Answers to these questions are vital if future policies are to result in more effective education of minority language children.

The Puerto Rican Community

The study has demonstrated that the Puerto Rican community, through a variety of interest groups and policy change strategies many years prior to the Aspira suit, sought to change educational policies determining the language of instruction and other practices in public school in Puerto Rico and the continental United States. In New York City the community was only marginally successful. Though many bilingual educational programs were implemented in the late 1960s, these addressed the needs of only a fraction of children of limited English-speaking ability. Despite the growing political power of the Hispanic community on a national level and increased federal policies in support of bilingual education, it was not until the consent decree was implemented in New York City schools that policy was changed to encompass a substantial number of Hispanic children of limited English-speaking ability.

In three respects, however, the consent decree did not respond to policy issues which Aspira of New York had intended to pursue. First, Aspira and the PRLDEF brought the suit on behalf of 182 thousand children. Only 58 thousand who were described as having limited English-speaking ability were ultimately entitled to the bilingual consent degree program. What happened to the remainder of the class? These were children who Aspira acknowledged had a knowledge of English. However, the agency maintained that because of the board of education's past failure to offer these children access to educational materials and experiences, they had steadily fallen behind their peers. Aspira felt that children in this category should be offered a program that would compensate for this perceived inequality of educational opportunity. Such a program would increase the pupil access to educational experiences and materials, give Puerto Rican children the opportunity to catch up with their peers, and offer the pupils the opportunity to participate in an enriched educational program which would strengthen and further develop their competence in their first language. Aspira maintained that the only program which could meet these objectives was a maintenance bilingual bicultural program. This program could not legally be construed as a pupil's right, since education is not a right. The lack of evidence and legal underpinnings for a case of liability rendered the issue unpursuable through the courts.

The need to continue to scrutinize policies for educating Hispanic children has recently been supported by a study conducted by the Education Commission of the States, National Assessment of Education Progress Project. It compared the achievement of Blacks, Whites, and Hispanics of three age levels—nine, thirteen, and seventeen—from 1970 to 1975. Specific skills studied were in the areas of science, mathematics, social studies, and career and occupational development. The study found that Hispanic students in the Northeast, with New York City students forming the majority of this group, lagged behind Hispanic students in the West in all but one area. The most critical deficits in achievement for Hispanic students in the Northeast were in the areas of social studies and mathematics, in which they scored eighteen and seventeen percentage points respectively below the national average. This is alarming when one notes that the sample studied included only Hispanic students who were identified as English proficient. On a national level, Hispanics in the Northeast consistently scored below both Hispanics in the West and Blacks, in the areas of science and social studies. In reading, this was also the case at ages nine and thirteen. A commentary on the data incorporated in the report concluded that

> Hispanic students do not receive equal benefits from the educational system of this country. The mere availability of public education is simply not enough. ... The data raise questions about the effectiveness of school systems as they presently exist to meet the needs of minority students.

> According to the National Assessment data, the deficits in achievement
> for Hispanos have not changed in the last six years. Hispanic students
> appear no closer to equal benefits in 1975 than they were in 1971.[38]

Aspira's position that maintenance bilingual bicultural educational programs may serve to equalize opportunity is only one of a few limited proposals.[39] While there is much resistance to bilingual education, educational
researchers and planners simply have not developed alternative approaches
that have demonstrated a positive impact. To obtain on the local level policy
reform that would encompass Puerto Rican children who are ineligible for
the consent decree program would require using other than litigation
strategies. These might include organizing efforts to bring about the reform
of administrative or legislative policies governing state compensatory funds
under Title I, Urban Education, and other education aid programs. This
would require scrutinizing and redefining such terms as *giftedness*. There
would seem to be a resistance to define bilingualism in any but a compensatory context. Funds for the gifted, for instance, could encompass bilingual
children in the definition of the population eligible to receive these funds.
Gifted children's bilingualism would then be viewed as an asset and programs could serve to nurture bilingual skills.

Another strategy for community input in policy determination must
include the community's organizing efforts to obtain representation on
community school boards. This is an important mechanism for community
participation. Other powerful and influential groups, such as the United
Federation of Teachers, have organized and obtained influence through
school elections. Yet another strategy may require that the community
support empirical research in linguistics to determine whether children
suffer irreparable linguistic or cognitive handicaps when educated under
traditional immersion or English as a second language approaches.

The second policy issue that Aspira sought unsuccessfully to address
was the question of the right of Puerto Ricans to maintain the Spanish
language whether they are on the island or the continental United States.
Knowledge of English is viewed as necessary and desirable by the children,
parents, educators, and leadership in the New York City community. The
issue is not the desirability of one language as opposed to the other but
rather whether the Puerto Rican should be required to give up one for the
other. Aspira has taken the position that since Puerto Ricans are U.S. citizens
and since the official language of Puerto Rico is Spanish, educational policies
in the continental United States should more adequately reflect and respond
to these realities. Aspira has argued that mainland public educational
systems in which there are significant numbers of Puerto Rican children
should adopt policies that provide the opportunity to learn English effectively while maintaining Spanish language skills. This policy issue, however,
is most directly related to the political status of Puerto Ricans and to the
nature of the agreement that established the commonwealth status of the

island. For the Puerto Rican, the future resolution of this issue may more appropriately lie on the federal legislative and political level rather than in the courts.

The third area in which Aspira sought policy reform was reflected in its goal to obtain a bicultural program for the class of children bringing the suit. This study's research base related to biculturalism was too sparse to argue that culture had to be a component of the remedy to which children were entitled. The board of education strongly resisted the notion that it was obligated to reinforce or even relate to the cultural heritage and ethnicity of minority language children. The only agreement that both parties could reach was that, wherever possible, the materials used in the program would reflect the culture of the children and would avoid negative stereotyping. The issue of whether public educational institutions should be required to adopt policies that are supportive of maintaining a child's ethnic identity has continued to be the subject of much debate. This controversy has emerged most strongly on the federal level.

Another issue that must be addressed here is the viability of the courts as mechanisms for ensuring the rights of minority groups. Though the suit was effective in obtaining a bilingual educational program for children who were being deprived of access to educational experiences and could, therefore, be viewed as an effective change agent, the question is whether the community really has access to the court system, in light of the magnitude of the cost of the litigation. In the *Aspira* case, for instance, how long can two nonprofit community agencies like Aspira and the PRLDEF continue to infuse the funds, efforts, and resources necessary to remain abreast of the program's implementation and to perform functions such as consultations and litigation?[40] Though on two occasions the PRLDEF has been awarded attorney's fees, these have not fully compensated the agency for its investment of resources in the suit.[41] Neither has Aspira been compensated for any of its efforts in bringing out the suit, maintaining a complaint system, responding to requests for information and orientation, monitoring compliance with the decree, analyzing voluminous reports on the program submitted by the Board, or other functions associated with representing the class of children bringing the suit. Aspira maintains that between 1970 and 1976 the agency has invested a substantial sum in carrying out responsibilities related to the suit. To carry out the major efforts of program monitoring, both Aspira and the PRLDEF continue to expend their limited resources and to depend on the voluntary support of individuals and groups in the field. These include teachers, students, administrators, parents, and community organizations which act as a network of information. The law does not provide a mechanism for reimbursement of expenses, other than attorney's fees, to such nonprofit community efforts in civil rights litigation.

In addition, what leverage do the courts offer minority groups? How meaningful are administrative or court threats to withdraw a school system's federal aid? Such action would adversely affect the best interest of the very children whom agencies like Aspira and the PRLDEF seek to represent and defend, inasmuch as they are often members of the population served by federally aided programs. On the one hand, the notion that substantial leverage can be wielded by withdrawal of what could amount to millions of dollars in federal aid is supported by the controversial minority hiring plan agreed to by the Office of Civil Rights (OCR) and the Board. On the other hand, some districts have been prepared to lose federal assistance rather than comply with OCR guidelines and regulations. District 1 refused to accept Title VII funds in 1975–76 as part of a controversy over the implementation of the consent decree program.

It would seem, then, from a community perspective, that the courts are a possible ally in policy change. However, there are many limitations to this approach in terms of the community's access because of the financial burden involved and because of the limitations in the purview and powers of the courts. Courts most often make judgments based on the letter and interpretation of existing laws and are reluctant to enter the pedagogical decisions of school authorities. Finally, the courts are frequently inappropriate arenas in which to discuss the ideal programs and policies which a community may seek to implement.

NOTES

1. The term *minority language children* includes all children who, as a function of membership in a minority ethnic group whose culture is identified and transmitted by one or more languages, speak a language other than, but not necessarily to the exclusion of, English.

2. The term *children of limited or no English proficiency,* as used by the author (and not necessarily in citations from other authorities), includes children whose first language is a language other than English and who speak, read, write, or understand English to a limited extent or not at all.

3. The term *children of Spanish-speaking background,* as used by the author, is a more specific yet inclusive term in that it refers to a particular minority language group, yet it is more specific than such terms as *Spanish speaking* or *Spanish surnamed.* Not all Spanish speakers belong to an ethnic minority group. Similarly, not all Spanish-surnamed individuals are necessarily of a Spanish-speaking background or ethnic group.

4. For the most recent national studies, see U.S., Commission on Civil Rights, *Mexican American Study,* 5 vols. (Washington, D.C.: U.S. Government Printing Office, 1971-1974); idem, *Puerto Ricans in the Continental United States: An Uncertain Future, October 1976* (Washington, D.C.: U.S. Government Printing Office, 1976), pp. 92-133.

5. Theodore Andersson and Mildred Boyer, *Bilingual Schooling in the United States,* 2 vols. (Austin, Tex.: Southwest Educational Development

Laboratories, 1970); and National Puerto Rican Development and Training Institute, "A Proposed Approach to Implement Bilingual Education Programs: Research and Synthesis of Philosophical, Theoretical, and Practical Implications," photocopied material (New York, 1972).

6. Comprehensive bibliographies of materials include Center for Applied Linguistics, *A Bibliography of American Doctoral Dissertations in Linguistics, 1900-1964* (Arlington, Va.: Center for Applied Linguistics, 1968); idem, *Reference List of Materials for English as a Second Language* (Arlington, Va.: Center for Applied Linguistics, 1964, 1966, 1969); idem, *Spanish and English of United States Hispanos: A Critical Annotated Linguistic Bibliography* (Arlington, Va.: Center for Applied Linguistics, 1975); and William F. Mackey, *International Bibliography on Bilingualism*, a computerized selection of over 11 thousand titles (Quebec: Les Presses de l' Université Laval, 1972).

7. Meyer Weinberg, *Minority Students: A Research Appraisal* (Washington, D.C.: U.S. Government Printing Office, 1977), p. 285.

8. U.S., Department of Health, Education, and Welfare, National Institute of Education, *Multilingual-Bicultural Division: Fiscal Year 1976 Program Plan* (cited from Aspira of New York files), p. 8 (hereinafter cited as NIE, *Program Plan*).

9. The term *consent decree* is defined as an agreement "entered by consent of the parties; it is not properly a judicial sentence, but is in the nature of a solemn contract or agreement of the parties, made under the sanction of the court, and in effect an admission by them that the decree is just determination of their rights upon the real facts of the case, if such facts have been proved." *Black's Law Dictionary*, 4th ed. (St. Paul, Minn.: West Publications, 1968), p. 499.

10. *Aspira of New York et al. v. Board of Education of the City of New York et al.*, 72 Civ. 4002 S.D.N.Y. 1974 (MEF) (hereinafter cited as "Aspira" in footnotes and as *Aspira* in the text).

11. Ibid., Consent Decree at para. 2 (S.D.N.Y. 29 August 1974), unreported (hereinafter cited as "Aspira, Consent Decree").

12. Aspira of New York, Inc., *Annual Report, 1965*, p. 3.

13. Ibid., p. 1.

14. Ibid., p. 10.

15. Ibid., p. 10.

16. Aspira of New York, Inc., *Decade of Achievement: ASPIRA Tenth Anniversary* (New York: Aspira, 1971), p. 10.

17. Aspira of America, *Annual Report 1974-75* (New York: Aspira of America, 1976), pp. 20-28.

18. Though programs and services are designed expressly for Puerto Ricans, any youth requesting such assistance is served by the agency.

19. Aspira of New York, Inc., *Annual Report 1974-75* (New York: Aspira of New York, 1976), p. 7.

20. Complaint at para. 1. 72 Civ. 4002 (S.D.N.Y. 20 September 1972) (hereinafter cited as Aspira, Complaint).

21. The suit was initially filed by thirteen individually named children and their guardians against authorities of their respective local school boards and the Central Board of Education of the City of New York. A motion was filed later that instituted the class action against the Board and all community school boards in New York City.

22. Aspira, Complaint at para. 2. The "class of children" refers to those children similarly situated to the individually named plaintiffs. Ibid., at para. 4-9.

23. Ibid., at para. 37.

24. Ibid., at para. 2.

25. Ibid., at para. 66. The term *bilingual education* as defined by *Bilingual Education Act of 1967, Statutes at Large* 81, sec. 703 (1968), *U.S. Code,* vol. 20, sec. 880b (1968) is "the use of two languages of instruction." Aspira later defined bilingual education as "a program of instruction which utilizes two languages in the curriculum which contains all four of the following components: (1) first language is reinforced and developed; (2) curriculum content areas are taught in a language the child fully comprehends; (3) English as a second language is taught in a sequentially structured program; (4) Puerto Rican culture is taught and reflected in all aspects of the curriculum." Plaintiff's Memorandum of Law at 3-16, 72 Civ. 4002 (S.D.N.Y. 20 May 1974), unreported memorandum.

26. Aspira, Consent Decree at para. 2.

27. Ibid., at para. 1.

28. Ibid., at para. 7, 10.

29. Ibid., at para. 11, which required that the Board "consult with plaintiffs with respect to the development of all items contained in the Consent Decree." The term *consultation* is, of course, a vague one and the difficulties and limitations of Aspira's exercising this prerogative are discussed in Chapter 3 of this study.

30. NIE, *Program Plan,* p. 3.

31. J. Stanley Pottinger, Director, Office of Civil Rights, U.S. Department of Health, Education, and Welfare, "Memorandum to School Districts with more than Five Percent National Origin-Minority Group

Children, Subject: Identification of Discrimination and Denial of Services on the Basis of National Origin." *Federal Register,* vol. 35 (25 May 1970), p. 11595.

32. Civil Rights Act of 1964, Title VI, *Statutes at Large 68,* sec. 252 (1964), *U.S. Code,* vol. 42, sec. 2000d (1970).

33. *Lau v. Nichols,* 414 U.S. 563 (1974) (hereinafter referred to as "Lau" in footnotes and *Lau* in the text).

34. Pottinger, DHEW, Memorandum, 25 May 1970, directed to "School Districts with more than Five Percent National Origin-Minority Group Children."

35. J. Stanley Pottinger, Summary in Lieu of Testimony, in U.S., Commission on Civil Rights, *Hearing: New York, February 14-15, 1972* (Washington, D.C.: U.S. Government Printing Office, 1972), pp. 725-737.

36. Civil Rights Act of 1964, Title VI, *Statutes at Large 68,* section 252 (1964), *U.S. Code,* vol. 42, section 2000d-1 (1970).

37. The remainder of the original class of 182 thousand children were not found to be entitled to the consent decree program.

38. Education Commission of the States, National Assessment of Educational Progress Project, *Hispanic Student Achievement in Five Learning Areas: 1971-1975* (Washington, D.C.: U.S. Government Printing Office, 1977), p. 31.

39. There are many models for bilingual education. However, in terms of other models for educating children of limited English proficiency, the two other approaches which have been implemented and tested broadly are English as a Second Language (ESL) and language immersion programs. Neither could be shown effective in educating Puerto Rican children in New York City schools.

40. An appropriate reminder here is that the legal process is demanding of plaintiffs in this type of case in that the burden of proof is on them and also because the courts are generally reluctant to interfere in public institutional authority unless "substantial" wrong is demonstrated.

41. 65 F.R.D. 541 (S.D.N.Y. 1975), and Aspira, Contempt Opinion, at 33 and at ii.; and interview with Peter Beinstock, Attorney, Puerto Rican Legal Defense and Educational Fund, New York, 4 November 1977.

☆ U.S. GOVERNMENT PRINTING OFFICE: 1981 — 727-678/1678 REGION 3-1